CHAPTER I

GENERAL DIRECTIONS FOR CANDY-MAKING

We find it quite possible to make just as delicious candy at home as can be bought of the most famous manufacturers. Of course there are a few kinds of candies that can be made only with the aid of special machinery; but there are enough kinds that can be made with utensils found in the ordinary kitchen (with a few more added) to make all the variety that one may wish for. By making our own candies in the home we have the assurance that they are at least pure and clean, and that they will cost us no more than the cheaper grades of candy. Candy-making is very fascinating, and there is no reason whatever why one cannot be a successful candy-maker after a few trials at it. In this first chapter we give a few general directions in candy-making that will make it easier to carry out all the recipes that follow.

Utensils

All the utensils that are needed in candy-making are saucepans of granite or porcelain, a double boiler, spoons, a spatula, candy dipper, platter or marble slab, a thermometer, and boxes or pans in which to mold certain kinds of candies. Bonbon molds are useful for molding bonbons, but are not necessary as they can easily be molded with the fingers. A thermometer is not absolutely necessary since one can learn to get the different stages by dropping and testing the syrup in cold water; but the thermometer makes it much easier to get the syrup cooked to exactly the right degree. In buying a thermometer choose one that is guaranteed by its maker, since some thermometers are apt to break when the syrup is boiled to a high degree as it must be in making the hard candies. There are small, reliable candy thermometers on the market that do not cost a great deal, and make it much easier for the candy-maker.

While a platter can be used instead of a marble slab in making fondant and some other candies, yet, since the marble is naturally cool, the candy syrups will cool much more quickly on it and for this reason is desirable.

In making taffies or any candy that requires pulling a hook is very useful. One can handle more at a time with a hook and pulling makes it lighter and nicer.

A sugar scraper proves very useful when it comes to scraping down maple sugar and chocolate; and a food chopper is very convenient when chopping nuts and fruits used in candy-making.

A smooth piece of tin can be used for dropping or placing the candies on, after they are made to set and cool; but paraffine paper will take its place very well. One can scarcely get along without this paper in candy-making, for it is very useful in lining candy-boxes when they are to be used as molds, and candies or bonbons that are liable to become sticky can be wrapped in it. A few bowls for dipping purposes will be needed.

Ingredients

Granulated sugar is the kind most frequently used in candy-making. To get the best results it should be fine-grained and of the best quality. Confectioner's sugar or powdered sugar is used chiefly to roll or dust candies with.

Almost all confectioners use glucose in their candies, since it helps to keep the sugar from granulating, but, since corn syrup is composed largely of glucose it is advisable for the home candy-maker to use it as it can be readily obtained at the grocery store. A few recipes call for glycerine, and this is quite harmless, and helps to make the candy smooth and creamy. Cream of tartar, vinegar and lemon juice are used to prevent the sugar from graining also.

The butter used in making butter-scotch, fudges and such like candies should be of the very best quality. Never under any circumstances use in candy, stale butter, or substitutes, or butter that is very salty.

A Few Things the Candy-Maker Should Know

230 to 235 degrees		Thread stage.
238 to 240	"	Soft ball stage.
250 to 255	"	Hard ball stage.
280 to 290	"	Crack stage.
300 to 310	"	Hard crack stage.

In testing the syrup with the thermometer allow the thermometer to become hot gradually.

If one does not have a thermometer and has to test the syrup in cold water one will have to depend a great deal on sight and touch. The thread stage is found by letting a little syrup drop from a spoon; if it forms a thread then it is known as the thread stage. The soft ball stage is reached when the syrup forms a soft ball between the fingers when dropped in cold water, and the hard ball stage is reached when it makes a firm ball between the fingers when dropped in cold water. The crack stage is reached when it cracks or becomes brittle, and the hard crack stage is reached when all the water has evaporated and the syrup is about ready to burn. At this stage one must watch it very closely.

After the sugar has melted when put over the fire, wipe the sides of the kettle down carefully; this removes the undissolved sugar, which is apt to cause the rest to grain if not removed.

All scum should be carefully removed as soon as the syrup boils; but be careful not to stir the syrup or jar it any more than possible. Candies in which milk, cream or chocolate is used should be boiled in a deep vessel as they have a tendency to boil over. Sugar and water and corn syrup will not boil over, so that the depth of the vessel in which they are boiled does not matter so much.

Hard candies should be loosened up from the tin, or whatever they are molded in, before they are quite cool, or they will stick and be hard to remove. It is well to remember that nearly all hard candies will become sticky in warm weather, so should be kept in glass jars or wrapped in waxed paper.

If a batch of candy should become grainy and go back to sugar again it can be boiled over, adding a little more water and corn syrup or cream of tartar; but do not use the same vessel unless it has been well washed.

The Coloring and Flavoring

Use nothing but fruit or vegetable colorings for candy; these can usually be obtained at a drug store, or from the confectioner. A little of these will go a long way. Colorings can be obtained in liquid form or in form of paste. The useful colors are orange, yellow, red, leaf green and violet. With red one can get all the shades of pink, and rose. Different shades of green can be made with the green by the amount used. Always remember that high colors are not desirable in candy and confine yourself to the paler shades as much as possible. You can obtain different shades by combining two colors; for instance, put a drop or two of red with your violet and you will have another shade, and so on. A good shade can be made with strong coffee.

By using different flavoring extracts one may have a great variety in candy. Use only pure extracts or oils. When using oil of peppermint or oil of cinnamon for flavoring remember it is very strong and use only a few drops, while from a half teaspoonful to a tablespoonful of extract may be used, according to the strength of flavoring desired. Always add the flavoring after the syrup has been removed from the fire, as in most cases it will boil out if put in with the other ingredients.

CHAPTER II

THE MAKING OF FONDANT

The foundation for innumerable cream candies and for nearly all bonbons is what the confectioners call "fondant." This is quite easily made by the home candy-maker after once getting the knack of it; but one must be careful to follow directions closely and not become careless. It has a great advantage from the fact that it can be made up a long time before it is worked into candies, since it will keep for a great length of time. It can be made up in large quantities, but it is best for the amateur candy-maker at first to make it in small quantities at a time, and make it oftener; then as she becomes more adept she may use several pounds of sugar at a making.

Fondant

To make the fondant take two pounds of granulated sugar, one-half cupful of water and one-fourth teaspoonful of cream of tartar. Boil this to the soft ball stage or to 238 degrees. Stir the sugar over a slow fire until it is thoroughly dissolved; then take a damp cloth and wipe away all the sugar crystals that appear on the sides of the pan. When it is done remove from fire and pour over a large platter that has been cooled or over a marble slab. Do not scrape the contents out of pan or allow it to drip, but pour out quickly, then there will be less danger of its graining. Let stand until nearly cool (not cold), then stir until it becomes thick and creamy, working it away from the edges of the platter or slab into a mass in the center. Use a wooden spoon in creaming the fondant, and it is a good idea to sprinkle a little cold water over the top of the syrup after it has been poured out on the platter; this will prevent a crust from forming on top. When too stiff to work with spoon take it in the hands and knead until it is smooth and velvety. Let stand a few hours until it has mellowed somewhat, then pack down in jars and bowls, and cover with a damp cloth. If kept for some time dampen the cloth occasionally. As we said before this fondant will keep for a long time, and one may use it when desired. If a batch should turn grainy after stirring it can be boiled over again, or used in making some other candy, but in either case it must be boiled over again and a little more water added. In making fondant it is best to take a kettle that has not been used for other purposes, or it will give the fondant a taste; also be very careful to have the thermometer clean if one is used. The fondant can be colored and flavored when still warm, or it can be colored and flavored when you warm or melt it when ready to make the bonbons. Fondant should cool quickly after it has been poured out on a platter or slab. As marble is naturally cool it is best for this purpose, but a platter may be placed on ice, or dipped in cold water before being used.

Chocolate Fondant

The above directions are for white fondant, which is the kind most generally made, but one can make chocolate and maple fondant. To make the chocolate fondant take two cupfuls of sugar and four ounces of grated chocolate and one-half cupful of water. Boil to the soft ball stage, flavor with a teaspoonful of vanilla and proceed as when making white fondant. It is best not to add the chocolate until the syrup has boiled a while, then it can be melted and slowly added, for the syrup must not be stirred while boiling.

Maple Fondant

To make maple fondant take one cupful of brown sugar and two cupfuls of maple syrup, or one cupful of maple sugar. If the sugar is used add one-half cupful of water. To keep the syrup from graining add one-fourth teaspoonful of cream of tartar. Boil to the soft ball stage or to 238 degrees by the thermometer, and then pour out on platter or slab, and proceed as with the white fondant. A good substitute for maple fondant may be made by flavoring with mapleine some of the white fondant. Maple fondant is especially good combined with nuts in making bonbons, and also makes nice centers for chocolate creams.

In the chapter on <u>bonbons</u> you will find many ways in which the fondant can be used, and many other ways will no doubt suggest themselves to you when you once begin to work with it.

CHAPTER III

HARD CANDIES

Many persons prefer the hard candies to the soft varieties. Most of these hard candies are boiled to the crack stage or hard crack stage, which is from 280 to 310 degrees. In testing these candies in cold water it is always advisable to remove from the fire while doing so, for when the syrup gets to the turning stage it will burn very soon if not watched. Other hard candies will be found classified under the chapter on nut candies, such as peanut brittle, nut nougats, etc.

Chocolate Chips

Place in a saucepan one cupful of brown sugar, one-half cupful of New Orleans molasses (the light colored molasses), and one tablespoonful of butter. Boil to the crack stage, then remove from the fire and flavor with one teaspoonful of vanilla. Pull into long thin sheets, and cut into small pieces. When cold dip into melted chocolate flavored with a little vanilla.

Cinnamon Jibb

Place in a saucepan one cupful of golden corn syrup, one-fourth cupful of butter, a tablespoonful of cinnamon, and one-half cupful of water. Boil to the crack stage. Pour into buttered pans, and mark off into squares. When cool break up.

Fig Brittle

Take two cupfuls of light brown sugar, one cupful of golden corn syrup and one-half cupful of water. Cook to the crack stage, and then stir in figs that have been cut up into bits. Pour into a buttered pan, and mark off. When cool break up. Date brittle can be made in the same manner.

Butter-Scotch

Take two cupfuls of light brown sugar, one-half cupful of butter, one-fourth cupful of water and one tablespoonful of vinegar. Boil to the crack stage. Pour into buttered tins, mark off into squares, and when cool break up. A tablespoonful or two of molasses improves butter-scotch for many persons.

French Butter-Scotch

Take two cupfuls of granulated sugar, one-half cupful of maple sugar, one-half cupful of butter, one tablespoonful of vinegar, and one-fourth cupful of water. Cook to the crack stage or to 280 degrees, then remove from fire and add one teaspoonful of vanilla, and one-fourth teaspoonful soda. Mark into strips, and when cold cut with a pair of shears.

Maple Panocha

Take one cupful of maple sugar, one cupful of light brown sugar, two tablespoonfuls of butter, and one-half cupful of water. Boil to the crack stage. Pour over pecan meats that have been placed on a buttered pan. When cold break in any manner desired.

Horehound Candy

Take two cupfuls of brown sugar, one cupful of corn syrup, and one-half teaspoonful of cream of tartar. Pour over this the horehound liquid made by steeping two ounces of dried horehound (which can be obtained at the drug store) in one pint of hot water. Boil down to a cupful before adding to the sugar. If you do not wish it to be very strong of horehound don't use quite so much. Boil to the hard crack stage or about 300 degrees. Pour into a buttered pan or pans. Mark deeply into small squares while still warm, and when cool it will break easily.

Chocolate Taffy

Take two cupfuls of sugar, one cupful of golden corn syrup, one-half cupful of boiling water, and one-fourth teaspoonful of cream of tartar. Boil to the soft ball stage, then add two ounces of unsweetened chocolate shaved fine. Boil to nearly the crack stage or about 270 degrees, then add one teaspoonful of vanilla. Pour out on a buttered platter, cool and pull. Cut into small pieces, using shears or sharp knife, and place on buttered plate or paraffine paper.

Molasses Taffy

Take two cupfuls of sugar, and one-half cupful of New Orleans or baking molasses, and one-half cupful of corn syrup, and a third teaspoonful of cream of tartar. Boil to about the crack stage. Turn out on a greased platter, and when cool enough pull until light colored. Cut in small pieces.

Nut Taffy

Take two cupfuls of light brown sugar, one-half cupful of corn syrup, one-half cupful of water, and one-fourth teaspoonful of cream of tartar. Boil to the hard ball stage. Add one teaspoonful of vanilla, and one cupful of nut meats, chopped. Pour out on a platter, and pull as soon as cool enough.

Lemon Stick Candy

Take two cupfuls of granulated sugar, one-half cupful of white corn syrup, one-half cupful of water, and the juice of one lemon. Boil all together with half the rind of the lemon to the crisp or crack stage. Flavor with one teaspoonful of extract of lemon, and color with yellow coloring. Pour out on a buttered platter, and when cool enough pull into sticks, and cut about four inches long.

Peppermint Stick Candy

Make the same as the lemon stick, but omit the lemon, and use one-fourth teaspoonful of cream of tartar. After removing from fire flavor with peppermint. Divide the candy into two portions, and color one with red coloring. Pull each part separately, then twist the red candy around the white till you have it in form of a stick. Cut into sticks, and if desired form into canes.

Strawberry Drops

Take two cupfuls of granulated sugar, one-half cupful of corn syrup, the juice of one lemon, and a fourth cupful of water. A tablespoonful of vinegar can be used instead of lemon juice if desired. Boil to the hard crack stage. Color with red coloring and flavor with strawberry flavoring. Drop from a spoon in drops about the size of a nickel onto waxed or greased paper. By flavoring with different flavoring and using different colorings you may have a variety in these drop candies.

Honey Peppermint Tablets

Take one cupful of honey, one cupful of sugar and one-half cupful of white corn syrup, one-fourth teaspoonful of cream of tartar and one teaspoonful of butter. Boil to the crack stage, then remove from fire and add one teaspoonful of peppermint extract. Drop from a spoon onto oiled paper, about the size of a nickel or quarter. This candy can be pulled if preferred, and cut into pieces.

Maple Tablets

Melt together in a saucepan one cupful of maple sugar and one cupful of light brown sugar, four tablespoonfuls of butter, one teaspoonful of lemon juice and one tablespoonful of water. Boil to the hard crack stage, and drop on oiled paper in drops about the size of a nickel. When partly cool stick two of the drops together.

Fruit Tablets

Take one cupful of sugar, one-half cupful of corn syrup and one-half glass of currant or any kind of jelly. Boil to the crack stage, add a teaspoonful of vanilla, almond or the kind of flavoring that goes best with the jelly used. Drop from a spoon on oiled or waxed paper, and when partly cool put two drops together.

Rose Nougat

Take two cupfuls of granulated sugar, one-half cupful white corn syrup, one-half cupful of water and a fourth teaspoonful of cream of tartar. Boil to the crack stage. Add one-half cupful of finely chopped candied cherries, and color a rose color with fruit or vegetable coloring. Let stand for a few moments until partly cool, then pour over the whites of two stiffly beaten eggs. Beat well and pour into a buttered mold. Cut into squares. One-half cupful of finely chopped almonds can be added if desired and flavored with one-half teaspoonful of almond extract.

Raisin Stickies

Take one cupful of sugar and one cupful of golden corn syrup and one cupful of finely chopped raisins, and one-half cupful of water and boil to the crack stage. Add one-half teaspoonful of cinnamon and one teaspoonful of vanilla. Pour into buttered pans, and when partly cool, mark off into sticks about an inch across. Twist each stick until twice the original length and cut in two. Place on paraffine paper until cool.

Vanilla Taffy

Place in a saucepan two cupfuls of white sugar, one cupful of white corn syrup, and one-half cupful of water. Bring to a boil, then add one teaspoonful of glycerine and a fourth teaspoonful of cream of tartar. Boil to about 260 degrees or to a little more than the hard ball stage and not quite to the crack stage. Pour on a greased platter or a slab, and add a tablespoonful of vanilla. Dip your hands in corn-starch and as soon as it cools enough to be handled pull until it is white and waxy. If a hook is used you can make nicer and whiter taffy. Remove from hands or hook and lay on waxed paper, and when cold break up; or it can be cut into small pieces while still warm. In summer taffy should be wrapped in waxed paper, since it is liable to become very sticky.

Salt Water Taffy

This is made the same as the vanilla taffy except that a tablespoonful of butter is added and one teaspoonful of salt. This can be flavored and colored to suit the taste and pulled like the vanilla taffy. In making taffy fold over the edges as it cools and keep folding the batch up until cool enough to pull.

Taffy Dreams with Nut Centers

Place in a saucepan two pounds of granulated sugar, one cup of water and one-half teaspoonful cream of tartar or a tablespoonful of lemon juice. Boil to the hard ball stage. Place some nut meats in a bowl and pour enough of the syrup over these so that they will be well coated. Set these in a cool place while pulling the remainder of the taffy. Put the syrup over the fire and boil until nearly the crack stage, then remove and flavor with vanilla or almond, or any flavoring desired. Pour over a large platter or a marble slab. Cool quickly, and then dip your hands in corn-starch and pull the candy until white. Form into a sheet about six inches wide while still warm. Lay on a tin or slab and spread the nut mixture in the center. Fold the edge of sheet over, pinch the edges together so that the nut part cannot be seen. Now stretch the candy by pulling it gently and quickly through the palms of both hands. Cut into pieces with a sharp knife and lay on waxed paper. Nut and fruit combined can be used for the centers, or fruit alone. In this case pour the syrup over them to make them stick together as above.

CHAPTER IV

FUDGES AND CARAMELS

Fudge is one of the most easily made, and one of the most popular of all the home-made candies. Caramels are also a favorite. These candies can be made a great variety of ways.

Chocolate Fudge

Take two cupfuls of sugar, two ounces of chocolate, one cup of good milk, and one tablespoonful of butter, or if you wish a richer fudge use two tablespoonfuls of butter. Bring the sugar, milk and butter to a boil and cook until it threads or to 235 degrees. Add the chocolate which should be melted or shaved fine. Stir it in well, then add a teaspoonful of vanilla, and beat up until creamy. The secret of good fudge lies in the beating. Some stir constantly from the time it is removed from the fire until it turns creamy, while others let it stand until nearly cool, and then beat up until creamy. Pour into buttered pan or mold, and when cold cut into neat small squares.

Maple Sugar Fudge

Take two cups of maple sugar, one cup of milk, one tablespoonful of butter, and one cupful of chopped walnut meats. Boil until the mixture forms a soft ball when dropped into cold water, or to about 240 degrees. Remove from fire and let stand until nearly cool, then stir until creamy. Pour into greased pans, and when cool cut into squares.

Burnt Almond Fudge

Brown blanched almonds in the oven and chop rather coarsely. Brown one-half cupful of granulated sugar in a granite pan; then add two-thirds cupful of milk, and when the browned sugar is thoroughly dissolved add one cupful of granulated sugar and one tablespoonful of butter. Boil until it makes a firm ball when dropped in cold water; flavor with almond extract and add one cupful of the browned almonds; stir until creamy, then pour into pans and mark off into squares.

COFFEE FUDGE

Take two cupfuls of granulated sugar, one cupful of strong boiled coffee, one-half cupful of cream and a teaspoonful of butter. Boil to the soft ball stage, then add a cupful of chopped nut meats, and stir until creamy. Pour into pans and cut into squares. The nuts may be omitted if desired.

MARSHMALLOW FUDGE

Take two cupfuls of light brown sugar, a cupful of milk, a tablespoonful of butter, and a fourth teaspoonful of cream of tartar. Boil until it threads or to 235 degrees, and then add a half pound of marshmallows. Beat until dissolved, add a cupful of chopped walnut meats. Pour into buttered pans and cut into squares. Another way to make this fudge is to omit the nuts and add two squares of chocolate.

PEANUT FUDGE

Take two cupfuls of brown sugar, one cupful of milk, and one teaspoonful of butter. When oily nuts are used in fudge one does not need to use so much butter. Boil to the thread or soft ball stage, and then add one cupful of finely ground peanuts and one teaspoonful vanilla. If preferred peanut butter may be used. Beat up until creamy, pour into buttered pans, and cut into squares.

FIG FUDGE

Take two cupfuls of granulated sugar, one cupful of water, a fourth teaspoonful of cream of tartar, one-half pound of figs, one teaspoonful of ginger, and one tablespoonful of butter. Boil the mixture to the soft ball stage. Remove from the fire and beat up until creamy. Pour into a buttered pan and mark into squares. Chop the figs before adding.

Divinity Fudge

Take two cupfuls of light brown sugar, add one-half cupful of golden corn syrup, and one-half cupful of water. Boil to the hard ball stage. Add one cupful of chopped walnut meats, and one teaspoonful of vanilla; and then pour over the stiffly beaten whites of two eggs. Beat up until light and foamy. Pour into buttered pans, and when cool mark off into squares.

Cocoanut Fudge

Take two cupfuls of granulated sugar, one cupful of milk, one tablespoonful of butter, and one-fourth teaspoonful of cream of tartar. Boil to the thread or soft ball stage and then add one cupful of grated cocoanut. Beat up until quite creamy.

Fruit Fudge

Take two cupfuls of light brown sugar, a cupful of milk, a tablespoonful of butter, and a pinch of cream of tartar. Boil until it makes a soft ball, then add a fourth pound of marshmallows. Beat until dissolved, then add one-half cupful of chopped walnut meats, and a cupful each of chopped dates and figs. Beat up until creamy, and pour into buttered pans.

Cinnamon Fudge

Take two cupfuls of light brown sugar, one cupful of milk, one-half cupful of butter, and two tablespoonfuls of cinnamon. Boil to the soft ball stage, remove from the fire and add a teaspoonful of vanilla. Beat up until creamy, pour into a buttered mold and cut into squares when cold.

Pineapple Fudge

Take two cupfuls of granulated sugar, one cupful of water, and a pinch of cream of tartar. Boil to the hard ball stage, then add one cupful of candied pineapple. Pour over the stiffly beaten whites of two eggs, and beat up until light and foamy.

Layer Fudges

These are fine and are made by pouring one kind of fudge upon another in layers. For this purpose one should use only the fudges that combine well together. Layers of several different kinds of fudge may be used, or only two, as desired. A chocolate fudge with a layer of divinity fudge between is delicious. Pour half of the chocolate fudge into a pan, and when cool pour over it a layer of divinity fudge; then when this has cooled pour over the remainder of the chocolate fudge which should have been kept hot in a bowl set in hot water. Fruit and nut fudges make a good combination.

Cocoanut Marshmallow Fudge

Take two cupfuls of sugar and one-half cupful of milk and boil up, then add one tablespoonful of butter and boil to the soft ball stage. Add a cupful of grated cocoanut and beat up until creamy. Arrange some marshmallows in a pan, and pour the fudge mixture over them. When cold cut into squares between the marshmallows.

Another Cocoanut Marshmallow Fudge

Take two cupfuls of granulated sugar, one cupful of milk and one tablespoonful of butter. Boil to the hard ball stage. Take it off the fire and add a teaspoonful of vanilla and one cupful of grated cocoanut. Mix this in, then add a half-dozen marshmallows. Let stand a while until soft; then pour the mixture over the stiffly beaten whites of two eggs. Beat up until it begins to get creamy, then pour into buttered pans, and when cool cut into squares.

Barley Fudge

Take a cupful of barley and brown it in the oven; be careful not to burn it, but have it a nice brown. Run this through the coffee-grinder. Take two cupfuls of brown sugar, one-half cupful of corn syrup, one-half cupful of milk and a tablespoonful of butter. Boil to the soft ball stage, add a tablespoonful of vanilla, then stir in the ground barley. Stir until creamy and pour out into a buttered pan, and when cold cut into squares.

Coffee Caramels

Take one cupful of light brown sugar, one cupful of golden corn syrup, one-half cupful of milk, one-half cupful of strong boiled coffee and one tablespoonful of butter. Boil to the hard ball stage. Remove from the fire, stir in one teaspoonful of vanilla, then pour into buttered pans, and mark off into squares. When cool cut into squares, and wrap each caramel in waxed paper.

Cocoanut Caramels

Take two cupfuls of granulated sugar, one-half cupful of white corn syrup, one-half cupful of cream, or if milk is used add one tablespoonful of butter. Boil to the hard ball stage. Remove from fire and stir in one cupful of grated cocoanut and one teaspoonful of vanilla. Pour into buttered pans, and when cold cut into squares.

Chocolate Caramels

Take one cupful of light brown sugar, one cupful of golden corn syrup, and one cupful of milk. Boil to about 235 degrees or to the soft ball stage, then add one-fourth pound of chocolate. Continue to boil to the hard ball stage or about 250 degrees. Flavor with vanilla, and pour into a buttered pan about an inch thick. Mark off into squares while still warm.

Sultana Caramels

Put into a saucepan two cupfuls of light brown sugar, one cupful of golden corn syrup, one-half cupful of milk and one-fourth cupful of butter. Bring to the boiling point, then add a cupful of Sultana raisins and one-half cupful of English walnut meats. Boil until it makes a firm ball when dropped into cold water or to about 250 degrees. Remove from the fire, add one teaspoonful of vanilla; pour into square greased pans to an inch or half-inch thick. Mark off into squares, and press a Sultana raisin in the top of each while still warm. When cold cut into squares.

Nut Chocolate Caramels

Place in a saucepan one cupful of brown sugar, one cupful of golden corn syrup, one-half cupful of milk and two tablespoonfuls of butter. Boil to the hard ball stage. Remove from the fire, add one teaspoonful of vanilla and one cupful of nut meats. Turn into square buttered pan, cool and cut into small squares, then dip into melted chocolate.

Vanilla Caramels

Take two cupfuls of sugar, one-half cupful of milk, and one-half cupful of golden corn syrup. Bring to a boil and then add two tablespoonfuls of butter. When nearly done add one square of chocolate. Boil to the hard ball stage, then flavor with a spoonful of vanilla. Pour into a square pan about an inch thick. Mark off in squares while still warm, and cut into cubes when cold.

Strawberry Caramels

Place in a saucepan one cupful of granulated sugar, one cupful of golden corn syrup and one tablespoonful of butter. Boil to the soft ball stage, then add one glassful of whole preserved strawberries, and boil until a hard ball will form between the fingers in cold water or to 250 degrees. Turn into a buttered pan, cool, and cut into small squares.

Jelly Caramels

Take two cupfuls of granulated sugar, one cupful rich cream, or if milk is used add a tablespoonful of butter, and one cupful of golden corn syrup. Boil to the hard ball stage then add a teaspoonful of vanilla, and pour into separate pans only about a third as thick as the usual caramels. Stiffen a glassful of any good jelly with a little gelatine melted in a little cold water. Pour this jelly when it begins to stiffen over one of the layers of caramel. Let stand until nearly cold, then remove the other layer of caramel from pan and place over the jelly. Let stand until perfectly cold, preferably over night, then cut into squares. Preserved fruits can be used instead of the jelly, and in this case, especially if the preserves are thick, no gelatine need be used.

Chocolate Cream Caramels

These are made in the same way as the above except that a layer of fondant is placed between the two layers of caramel. Melt the fondant, and pour over the caramel, and when barely cool place the other layer on top. Press lightly so that the layers will blend together. When cool cut into squares.

Molasses Caramels

Take one cupful of brown sugar, two cupfuls of New Orleans molasses, one-half cup of milk, and one-half cupful of butter. Boil to the hard ball stage, then remove from the fire, and add one teaspoonful of vanilla. Pour into a buttered pan, mark off into squares when partly cool, and when cold cut into cubes.

Franconia Caramels

Take one cupful of light brown sugar, one cupful of molasses, one cupful of milk and two tablespoonfuls of butter. Boil to the hard ball stage, then remove from fire and add one-half cupful of walnut meats, and a teaspoonful of vanilla. Turn into a buttered pan, and when cool cut into cubes, and dip each one in melted chocolate.

Tutti-Frutti Caramels

Take two cupfuls of light brown sugar, one cupful of golden corn syrup, one-half cupful of milk, one tablespoonful of butter, one-half cupful of chopped dates, one-half cupful of chopped figs, one-half cupful of chopped seeded raisins, and one-fourth cupful each of candied orange peel and citron. A half cupful of black walnut meats will improve this candy. Boil to the hard ball stage, stirring often to keep from sticking. Remove from fire, add a teaspoonful of vanilla, then pour into buttered pans, and mark off into squares.

CHAPTER V

NUT CANDIES

Many delicious candies may be made by adding nuts to the other ingredients, and since nuts have much food value these candies are healthful and nourishing.

Chocolate Almonds

Blanch a pound of almonds; this is done by pouring hot water over the almond meats and letting them stand on back of stove for about five minutes when the skins can easily be slipped off. Place on a pan in the oven and brown a nice dark brown, but be careful not to let them burn. When cool dip each almond in melted sweet chocolate.

Brown Almond Nougat

Blanch and cut one pound of sweet almonds in slices; lay them on a paper in a pan, and place in the oven until slightly brown. Take two cupfuls of granulated sugar, one-half cupful of golden corn syrup, and one teaspoonful of lemon juice. Melt to a liquid, stirring well, then add the almonds and mix well with the syrup. Butter a large platter or marble slab. Pour the nougat on this and make it even with a lemon, which should be lightly dipped in oil or melted butter. Make it about an inch thick, and cut into strips or bars, or it may be used to line molds. The molds are first slightly buttered on the inside, then a thin layer of nougat is pressed against the form; this must be done while the nougat is still warm. When cool turn out of form or mold, and these may then be filled with candied fruit and whipped cream, candies or ice-cream.

White Nougat

Boil two pounds of honey to the crack stage, or nearly to the crack, have the whites of four eggs beaten stiff, and add to the honey. Stir over a slow fire until it has reached the crack stage; then add two pounds of blanched almonds cut into strips and slightly browned in the oven. Mix all together and pour on platter or marble slab, or else line a nougat frame with wafer paper which can be bought at a confectionery shop, then pour the nougat into the frame, put board and weight on top.

Peanut Brittle

Take two cupfuls of light brown sugar, one cup of corn syrup, one-half cupful of water, one tablespoonful of butter and cook to the crack stage, then add a teaspoonful of vanilla, and two cupfuls of peanuts that have been slightly roasted, and stir until it begins to turn brown. Be careful not to let it burn, or become more than a golden brown in color. Add one tablespoonful (level) of soda, stirring it quickly, then pour over a greased platter or marble slab. As soon as it is thin enough to handle, loosen from the platter or slab with a knife, turn over and stretch out very thin. Break up into any desired shape when cold.

Almond Toffee

Take two cupfuls of brown sugar, two tablespoonfuls of butter and one-half cupful of cream and boil to the hard ball stage; then add one cupful of chopped almonds and one teaspoonful of vanilla. Boil to the crack stage. Pour into buttered pans, and mark off into squares.

Southern Hazelnut Toffee

Melt one-half cupful of butter in a saucepan, add one cupful brown sugar and one cupful New Orleans molasses. Boil to the hard ball stage, add one cupful of chopped hazelnuts and boil to the crack stage. Pour into buttered pan, and mark off into squares.

Mexican Panocha

Take two cupfuls of brown sugar, one-half cupful of corn syrup, one cupful of sweet milk, one teaspoonful of butter, and one square of chocolate. Mix the ingredients and boil to the hard ball stage, stirring the mixture constantly while on the stove. Add one cupful of pecan or any chopped nut meats, and pour into buttered pans. When cold cut into squares.

Pralines

Take two cupfuls of light brown sugar, one cupful of cream, and boil to the soft ball stage. Remove from fire and add one cupful of whole pecan meats, and one teaspoonful of vanilla. Stir until creamy, but be careful not to break the nut meats. A good way is to stir until it begins to cream, then add the nuts, and stir until the meats are well mixed with the creamy mass. Place in a cool place for a while, then separate the nut meats, keeping each one roughly coated with the cream candy.

Cream Nut Bars

Take two cupfuls of light brown sugar, one cupful of maple sugar, and one cupful of cream and boil to the soft ball stage. Remove from the fire and stir in one teaspoonful of vanilla, then stir until it begins to get creamy; add one cupful of finely chopped nut meats. Pour into a square pan, mark off into small squares, and press a half nut meat in center of each square. Cut into bars when cool, allowing two or three squares to a bar.

Maple and Butternut Cream

Take two cupfuls of maple sugar, and one cup of cream. Boil to the soft ball stage. Remove from the fire and add one cupful butternut meats, and stir until it turns creamy. Pour into buttered pans, and cut into squares. Maple and walnut creams may be made in the same manner. Place a half of a nut meat on top of each square.

Chocolate Nut Candy

Take two cupfuls of granulated sugar, one-half cupful of water, one-fourth teaspoonful of cream of tartar, and boil to the soft ball stage, then add one-fourth cupful of melted chocolate, one teaspoonful of vanilla and one cupful of nut meats. Beat up until creamy. Pour into buttered pans, and when cold cut into squares or bars. Peanuts, walnuts, pecans or any kind of nuts can be used for this candy.

Nut Bonbons

Take two cupfuls of granulated sugar, one-half cupful of white corn syrup, one-fourth teaspoonful of cream of tartar. Boil to the soft ball stage. Pour into four different plates. In one plate put a little melted chocolate and a fourth teaspoonful of vanilla, on another plate pour a few drops of red coloring and flavor with strawberry, on another plate pour a little yellow coloring and flavor with orange or lemon. Drop about a dozen almonds on each plate, the fourth plate being left white. Stir each plate until syrup is creamy, and each nut is well coated with the sugar. Separate each nut and place on waxed paper.

Candied Chestnuts

Take the chestnuts that are to be candied and score each nut on one side with a sharp knife. Cover with boiling water, cook five minutes and dry. Add a teaspoonful of butter to each pint of nuts, and stir or shake over the fire for five minutes. This loosens the shells and the inner skins, which can now be removed together. Cover the shelled nuts with cold water, and to each pound of nuts add the juice of one lemon. Let stand in this over night, since this will help to harden the nuts, so they can be boiled without breaking up. In the morning, drain, and simmer slowly for one or two hours, or until the nuts are tender. Make a syrup using a pound of sugar to each pound of nuts. Add to each two cupfuls of sugar a half cupful of water and cook until thick, add the nuts and simmer slowly for a half hour, then drain; let them stand in the syrup over night, removing them from the fire. The next day boil the syrup until thick as honey.

Remove the nuts and place on plates and set in the oven or in the sun to dry. Boil the syrup down a little thicker, and pour over the nuts several times while drying until all is absorbed. Dry the nuts and store between layers of waxed paper in a box.

Glacé Nuts

Take two cupfuls of granulated sugar, one-half cupful of water, and one-half teaspoonful of cream of tartar. Boil to the hard crack stage or until the syrup begins to turn brown. Add a teaspoonful of vanilla. Take the nuts to be dipped separately on a long pin, dip into the syrup to cover, remove and place on oiled or waxed paper. Almonds, walnuts, hazelnuts, pecans and peanuts can be used for dipping.

Walnut Bonbons

Place in a saucepan one cupful of granulated sugar, one-half cupful of golden corn syrup, one-half cupful of water, and a pinch of cream of tartar. Boil to the hard ball stage, then add one-half teaspoonful of vanilla and one-half cupful of English walnut meats chopped fine. Pour over the beaten white of one egg, and beat up until light. When it begins to harden drop on halved English walnut meats and press a half nut meat on the top of each bonbon.

Peanut Molasses Candy

Take one cupful of sugar, one cupful of New Orleans or sorghum molasses, and a tablespoonful of butter and boil to the hard crack stage. Stir in two cupfuls of peanuts, or just as many as you can, as the more nuts in this candy the better. Pour on a greased pan. When cold break into pieces or cut into squares with a very sharp knife.

Mexican Nut Confection

Take two cupfuls of light brown sugar, a quart of sweet milk and boil until the sugar is all melted, then stir in the well beaten yolks of six eggs. Boil until thick and smooth, stirring constantly, then add one pound of almonds that have been blanched and worked into a paste, and one teaspoonful of cinnamon. Boil to a firm mass, and stir to keep from sticking. This should be made in a double boiler. Pour into a buttered mold at least two inches thick, and when very cold slice. This is good dipped in chocolate or fondant.

Nut Loaf

Take an equal quantity of walnut, hickory-nut, almond and pecan meats and chop fine. To each cupful of nut meats have one-half cupful of chopped fruit, using dates, figs, raisins or candied cherries. Work the fruit and nuts well together. For each cupful of this mixture take one cupful of fondant. Melt the fondant, and stir the fruit and nut mixture into it; then remove and knead. Form this into an oblong loaf, flatten on top. Cover with paraffine paper and let stand for several days until the fruit and nuts are well blended with the fondant, then cut into slices.

Nut Stuffed Fruit

Dates are especially nice stuffed with nut meats. Remove the stones and insert a salted blanched almond in each, or chop up some walnut meats and work into a paste with a little cream or fondant and insert in the center of the dates. Close up and roll the dates in powdered sugar or else dip into fondant. Large prunes soaked over night until plump, and then stuffed with chopped almonds or pecan nut meats are fine. Large Sultana raisins are also good stuffed with nut meats.

Cherry and Almond Confection

Take two cupfuls of sugar, one-half cupful of corn syrup and a half cupful of milk and boil to the soft ball stage. Add a half cupful of chopped almonds, one-half cupful of candied cherries, and one teaspoonful almond extract. Stir until creamy, pour into buttered pan, and when cold cut into squares. Decorate some of the squares with almond meats and others with candied cherries.

FRUIT CANDIES

Some of the most delicious home-made candies are made with the addition of fruits to the other ingredients. All kinds of candied fruits, also many kinds of dried fruits, such as dates, figs, raisins and prunes may be used in candy-making. Many may not know that just as delicious candies can be made with our home-preserved fruits.

Candied fruits are in most cases expensive, but they can be made at home, and therefore the expense cut down. Cherries can be candied in the following manner: Select nice, large, and not over-ripe cherries for this purpose. Stone them carefully. Weigh the cherries, and to each pound of the fruit add two pounds of sugar, using only the best granulated for this purpose. Put the sugar in a kettle with one-half cupful of water, and boil to a thick syrup, removing all scum as it arises. Place a few of the cherries in at a time, and let simmer slowly until the fruit is transparent. Remove the fruit with a strainer, and add more of them until all have been cooked in this manner. Then place them back in syrup and let them stand over night in it. In the morning remove and place them out in the sun. It is a good idea to place them in a sieve, spreading them over it, and then cover the sieve with netting. They can be dried in the oven if desired, but one must be careful that they do not burn. When dried place in boxes between layers of paraffine paper, sprinkling each layer with powdered sugar. Place in a dry place until ready to use them in making candies. Pears, quinces, pineapples, peaches and plums may all be candied. Select firm-textured fruit and boil until tender in water before placing in the syrup; then proceed as in candying the cherries. Orange and lemon rind may also be candied. Remove the skin from the oranges or lemons in quarters and simmer in water until soft; then drain and remove all the white portion by scraping with a silver knife or spoon. Cut the oranges or lemons into small strips with the scissors, cook in the thick syrup, and roll in granulated sugar.

Quince Confections

Melt some fondant in a bowl, flavor with orange or lemon. Put some preserved quinces into the oven until dry. Dip each quarter into melted fondant. Place on oiled paper to dry. Preserved pineapple can be used in the same way.

Maraschino Drops

Take maraschino cherries. Dip into melted white or pink fondant that has been flavored with almond extract; then when hardened dip into melted chocolate fondant, or melted chocolate.

Strawberry Divinity Fudge

Place in a saucepan two cupfuls of granulated sugar, half a cupful of water and a fourth teaspoonful of cream of tartar. Boil to the hard ball stage. Add one glassful of whole preserved strawberries and boil up again. Pour the mixture over the stiffly beaten whites of two eggs and beat up until light and foamy. When the mixture begins to harden pour into buttered pans and when cool cut into squares. Any thick preserved fruits can be used in the same way. Preserved strawberries and preserved pineapple are good combined, half and half of each being used. If pear preserves are used a little chopped ginger will be an improvement.

Tutti-Frutti Cream

Melt one pound of fondant in a double-boiler, add one teaspoonful of vanilla or orange flavor; then add one tablespoonful of strawberry preserves (using only the berries), one tablespoonful of preserved cherries, two tablespoonfuls of preserved or candied pineapple, and one tablespoonful each of peach and pear preserves. The addition also of a teaspoonful each of candied orange and lemon peel will improve the mixture. When partly cool pour into a mold for slicing or form into bonbon shapes. If not quite stiff enough add powdered sugar to make of the right consistency to mold nicely. These can be rolled in powdered sugar or dipped in colored melted fondant or coated with chocolate.

Pear Caramels

Place in a saucepan two cupfuls of light brown sugar, one cupful of corn syrup, half a cupful of good milk and one tablespoonful of butter. Boil for a few minutes, then add one cupful of preserved pears, half a cupful of chopped candied ginger and a fourth cupful of candied lemon peel. Boil to the hard ball stage, add one teaspoonful of orange flavor and pour into pans. When cold cut into squares. Peach caramels are made in the same manner, only instead of the candied ginger a cupful of chopped almonds is added, the orange or lemon peel is omitted and almond extract used.

Marzipan Fruit Candies

Delicious fruit candies can be made by using marzipan paste. To make this paste take one cup of blanched almonds and run them through a food chopper; then pound to a fine flour. Place in a bowl and add to this flour the same amount of powdered sugar. Use enough water, rose water, orange juice or grape juice to make stiff paste—about three ounces will be enough. Beat an egg up stiff and work it into the paste. Roll out the marzipan an inch thick and cut into rounds or squares. Place a bit of preserved fruit on each one and mold the paste up around it. Place in the oven until the candies are dry. Another way to make the paste is to boil the ingredients. Use about three ounces of rose water or other liquid to the amount of almonds and sugar given above. Stir over a slow fire until when touched with the finger the syrup will cling. When cool knead into a paste.

Surprise Dates

Select some nice large dates and remove the stones. Fill some of the cavities with chopped raisins, figs, nuts and so forth, and some with chopped candied cherries; try to have the varieties of fillings as great as possible. Fondant with several different flavorings may also be used. Dip some of these stuffed dates in chocolate fondant, some in different colored fondants and some in plain white. Every date eaten then will prove to be a surprise and delight.

Marshmallow Fruit Fudge

Tear out a piece from the center of each marshmallow, being careful not to make a hole quite through it. Fill the cavities thus formed with any good preserved fruit. Make a chocolate fudge and pour it over the marshmallows, which should have been placed on greased paper in a pan. Be sure that the fruit is entirely covered. When cold cut out in cakes; they can be dipped in chocolate or left as they are. These are delicious and will prove an agreeable surprise to those who have never eaten them before.

Frosted Fruit Fudge

Make a good chocolate fudge, beating it until creamy, and pour it into a greased pan to about an inch in depth. When this is almost hard cover with any thick preserved fruit desired. Then place in a kettle one cup of granulated sugar, a fourth cupful of water and a pinch of cream of tartar. When the mixture has boiled to the hard ball stage pour it over the stiffly beaten white of one egg, add a teaspoonful of vanilla, or the kind of flavoring that will combine best with the fruit used, and beat up until light and foamy. Pour this over the fruit in the pan. When cold cut into squares, and you will have a delicious candy. Nut meats can be mixed in with the fruit. Almonds are also very good combined with peach preserves.

Cherry Foam

Place in a saucepan two cupfuls of granulated sugar, half a cupful of water and a fourth teaspoonful of cream of tartar. Boil until it forms a hard ball. Just before taking the syrup from the fire stir in a cupful of preserved cherries—the clear, transparent kinds are best. Pour the mixture over the stiffly beaten whites of two eggs and beat until light and foamy. Lay whole candied cherries two inches apart on waxed or greased paper and drop the foam by spoonfuls on these, pressing candied cherries on top of each. This candy is not only delicious but pretty to the eye as well.

Fig Favorites

Select the best quality of figs and steam until soft, then make an incision in each lengthwise and stuff with chopped nut meats. Close and place on a buttered pan. Boil together two cupfuls of sugar, one-half cupful of water, and one-fourth teaspoonful of cream of tartar. Boil until it will make a hard ball when dropped into cold water, flavor with a little vanilla, and then pour over the stuffed figs. When nearly cold mark off into squares, then dip in melted chocolate.

Pineapple Marshmallows

Soak four ounces of gum arabic in one cupful of pineapple juice until dissolved; then strain through cheese-cloth. Put into a saucepan with one-half pound of best powdered sugar and place saucepan in a pan of hot water on the stove. Stir the mixture until it becomes thick and white. Drop a little into cold water, and if it becomes a firm ball, remove from the fire and whip into it the stiffly beaten whites of three eggs. Flavor with a teaspoonful of vanilla. Dust a square pan with corn-starch and pour in the mixture until an inch thick. Let it stand in a cool place for twelve hours, then cut it into inch squares and roll in a mixture of powdered sugar and corn-starch.

Fruit Chocolate Balls

Take one cupful each of dates, seeded raisins and English walnut meats. Pass through a food chopper. Form into balls, and dip into melted chocolate fondant.

Watermelon Dainty

Take two cupfuls of sugar, one-fourth cupful of water, one tablespoonful of white corn syrup, and a pinch of cream of tartar and boil until it spins a thread or to 230 degrees. Pour over the stiffly beaten whites of two eggs, and beat up until light and foamy. Add one teaspoonful of vanilla, one cupful of chopped preserved watermelon rind, and one-half cupful of chopped nut meats. Color pink with a little red fruit or vegetable coloring. Pour into a buttered pan or mold to cool and cut into squares.

Date Delight

Take two cupfuls of light brown sugar, one cupful of milk, and one tablespoonful of butter. Boil to the soft ball stage. Add a teaspoonful of vanilla, and one cupful of chopped dates. Beat up until creamy. Pour into buttered pan or mold, and cut into squares when cold.

STUFFED PRUNES

Remove the stones from the prunes. Crack the stones and chop up the pits. Add the chopped pits to chopped dates, and fill the cavities of the prunes with the mixture. Dip the prunes in melted fondant. Another way to stuff the prunes is to stone some dates, fit a cherry inside of each date, then fit the date into the prune, and dip in the fondant. The prunes should be soaked in water for several hours before stuffing, and should be drained and wiped dry. Prunes filled with fondant or fondant and nuts mixed are also delicious.

FRUIT ROLL

Cook two cupfuls of brown sugar, one-half cupful of golden corn syrup and one-fourth cupful of water until it spins a thread. Remove from the fire and add the grated rind of one lemon and one orange, and a teaspoonful of the juice of each, one cupful of seeded raisins, one cupful of English currants, one-half cupful of cocoanut, one-half cupful of dates, and one-fourth cupful of figs; these fruits should all be run through a food chopper. Stir all until it forms a mass. Roll out into a thin sheet, and then roll up like a jelly roll, and cut into thin slices.

JELLY CAKE CANDY

Melt some fondant and pour into a square or round mold. Candy boxes lined with waxed paper will do. When cool place over this a thin layer of some thick jelly, such as currant, red raspberry, or orange; then pour over this another layer of fondant, and when this has cooled spread with another thin layer of jelly and pour over the top some more fondant. The layers of fondant may be colored differently if desired, and flavored to suit the jelly used. When cold turn out of mold, and cut into thin slices.

CHAPTER VII

SEA FOAM AND CREAM CANDIES

Sea foam and cream candies are delicious, and very easily made by the home candy-maker. Sea foam candies are those in which the white of egg is used, while the cream candies are made much after the same manner as fondant is made, except that cream is used instead of water.

Ginger Creams

Place in a saucepan two cupfuls of granulated sugar, one-half cupful of cream, one-fourth teaspoonful of cream of tartar or a few drops of acetic acid and one-half teaspoonful of glycerine. Boil until it forms a soft ball when dropped into cold water or to about 240 degrees; then pour the syrup on a large platter and when it has become slightly cool cover with candied ginger cut into thin strips—about one-half cupful will be enough. Work with a wooden spoon from the sides of the dish until it becomes creamy and smooth; then gather up in the hands and knead thoroughly. Roll out into a sheet and cut into thin bars, laying a strip of ginger on each bar and pressing it in with the finger.

Lemon Creams

Place in a saucepan one cupful of granulated sugar, one-half cupful of cream, the grated rind of one lemon. Boil to the soft ball stage; color with a few drops of yellow coloring and when slightly cool beat up until creamy. Form into bonbons and decorate with candied lemon peel.

Peppermint Creams

Place in a saucepan two cupfuls of granulated sugar, one-fourth cupful of white corn syrup, one-fourth teaspoonful of cream of tartar, and one-half cupful of cream. Boil to the soft ball stage. Let stand until nearly cool, then flavor with six drops of oil of peppermint, or one-half teaspoonful of extract, and add a few drops of red coloring to make a light shade of pink. Beat up until creamy and form into mint shape. Wintergreen creams can be made by flavoring with wintergreen.

Maple Creams

Place in a saucepan two cupfuls of light maple sugar and one-half cupful of cream. Boil to the soft ball stage, then stir in one cupful of finely chopped nut meats, and one teaspoonful of vanilla. Beat until creamy, and pour into a buttered pan. Cut into small squares. These are good dipped in melted chocolate.

Walnut Creams

Take two cupfuls of light brown sugar, one-half cupful of golden corn syrup, and one-half cupful of cream. Boil to the soft ball stage, add a cupful of finely chopped walnut meats, and a teaspoonful of vanilla. Beat until the mixture becomes creamy, then pour into buttered pan, and when cold mark off into small squares.

Cocoanut Creams

Take two cupfuls of granulated sugar, one-fourth cupful of white corn syrup, one-half cupful of cream, and one-fourth teaspoonful of cream of tartar. Boil to the soft ball stage, then add one teaspoonful of vanilla, and one-half cupful of shredded cocoanut. Stir until creamy, and pour into buttered pan. Can be formed in bonbon shape or poured into buttered pan.

Honey Creams

Take two cupfuls of granulated sugar, two tablespoonfuls of strained honey, and one-half cupful of water. Boil to the hard ball stage, then remove from fire and stir in one-half teaspoonful of almond extract, and a half cupful of chopped almonds. Pour over the stiffly beaten whites of two eggs.

Beat up until light and foamy, and drop from a spoon on greased paper. Decorate the top with almonds.

Vanilla Sea Foam

Take two cupfuls of light brown sugar, one-half cupful of water, and one-fourth teaspoonful of cream of tartar. Boil to the hard ball stage or to 250 degrees. Remove from the fire and flavor with one teaspoonful of vanilla, then pour over the stiffly beaten whites of two eggs. Beat up until light and foamy, and drop from a spoon on greased paper or a buttered plate. These are fine dipped in melted chocolate.

Maple Foam

Take two cupfuls of maple sugar, one cupful of brown sugar, one-half cupful of water, and a fourth teaspoonful of cream of tartar. Boil to the hard ball stage, then add a dozen marshmallows cut up into bits. Cover and let stand for five minutes, then pour over the stiffly beaten whites of two eggs. Beat up until light and it begins to harden. Drop from a spoon on greased paper, and place a half walnut meat on top of each piece of candy.

Candied Cherry Foam

Place in a saucepan two cupfuls of granulated sugar, one-half cupful of water and one-fourth teaspoonful of cream of tartar. Boil to the hard ball stage, and just before removing from the fire stir in a cupful of candied cherries cut into bits; then stir the mixture over the stiffly beaten whites of two eggs, add a few drops of red coloring, just enough to make a delicate pink, and beat up until light and it begins to harden. Drop from a spoon on waxed or greased paper, and garnish each drop with a candied cherry. This candy is not only pretty to the eye but delicious as well.

CHAPTER VIII

BONBONS

The foundation for nearly all bonbons is fondant. Hundreds of varieties of bonbons can be made by using different flavorings and different combinations of one kind with another. Bonbon making is fascinating work, and after they are made the home candy-maker has the satisfaction of knowing that she has a pure delicious candy at much less expense than if she bought it.

Chocolate Creams

Many may be surprised to know that they can make several hundred different varieties of chocolate creams alone. The simplest chocolate creams are made by dipping the plain fondant, after it has been formed in bonbon shapes, into melted chocolate. These fondant centers may be flavored with vanilla, peppermint, wintergreen, pineapple, orange, lemon, banana, almond, pistachio, cinnamon, allspice and clove, rose and other kinds of flavors found in the market. Certain kinds of flavors can also be combined, which helps to add to the variety. Maple chocolate creams are made by dipping maple fondant into melted chocolate. Plain fondant, chocolate fondant and maple fondant are all fine combined with nuts. All sorts of candied fruits, preserved fruits and dried fruits are delicious combined with fondant in making these creams. Candied peels and candied ginger are also much used.

Chocolate Creams With Fruit Centers

Maraschino cherries, drained and dipped first in melted fondant flavored with almond, and then coated with chocolate, are delicious.

Bits of candied pineapple dipped into fondant flavored with pineapple, lemon or orange and then coated with the chocolate, are fine.

Work some thick pear preserves into fondant, add a little chopped candied ginger, and when cool coat with chocolate. Or before coating them with chocolate dip in fondant flavored with lemon or vanilla.

Peach preserves dried in the oven, cooled and dipped in almond flavored fondant, then coated with chocolate, is another good combination.

Whole strawberry preserves, drained of all juice, rolled in powdered sugar, then coated with chocolate, are delicious.

Chopped candied cherries mixed into melted fondant either flavored with vanilla or almond, formed into bonbon shape, then coated with melted chocolate, are fine. Some of these cherry centers may be left white and red, or the fondant used can be colored rose and pink with a few drops of red fruit coloring.

Candied lemon rind, orange rind or citron can be cut up into small pieces, worked into fondant, and then coated with chocolate. Yellow fondant flavored with orange or lemon can be used with orange and lemon rind.

Stiff marmalades and jellies can be cut into fancy shapes, dipped into melted fondant of different flavors, and when cool coated with chocolate.

Dates and raisins chopped fine and worked into fondant make excellent centers. Mix some chopped dates with maple fondant for these centers. Chopped dates and chopped figs or raisins combined and worked into maple fondant are delicious.

California grapes dipped into melted fondant, and then into melted chocolate make another variety of creams.

Chocolate Creams with Nut Centers

Almonds, walnuts, pecans, hazelnuts, hickory-nuts, peanuts and Brazil nuts can all be used in making centers for chocolate cream candies. The nuts should be first blanched. Put two cupfuls of fondant in a double boiler and melt, add a teaspoonful of lemon juice, stir over the fire until melted; then take the nut meats, one by one, on a candy dipper or fork and dip into the fondant. Lay on oiled or paraffine paper until cold, then dip into melted chocolate. The fondant may be divided if preferred and flavored with different flavors, and prepared with different colors. Cherry flavored fondant is excellent with almonds. Vanilla goes well with most nuts, and many like peppermint flavor with nuts. Maple flavored fondant is always excellent with nuts.

Take equal quantities of chopped walnuts, hickory-nuts and almonds. These should be chopped fine. Take an equal amount of fondant and melt in a double boiler, and stir in the nut meats; flavor with vanilla if the fondant has not already been flavored. When the fondant mixture begins to harden mold into bonbon shape, and place on paraffine paper or a sheet of clean tin. When entirely cool coat with chocolate.

Delicious bonbons can be made by grinding up pistachio nuts until fine, and mixing with an equal quantity of pale green or white fondant flavored with pistachio or almond. When cool enough shape in bonbons, and coat with chocolate.

Chop equal quantities of almond nut meats and candied cherries, or preserved cherries. Mix with a little fondant, roll into balls and coat with chocolate, and you have a delicious cream.

Take walnut meats and dip in melted fondant, and when this has become firm dip in more fondant of a different flavor and color. Repeat this twice, then when cold coat with chocolate. Any kind of nut meats may be used in the same way.

How to Coat Chocolate Creams

Most confectioners use a bittersweet chocolate with which they coat their chocolates; this may be obtained at any good confectionery shop and will cost about fifty cents a pound, but if this is not obtainable a bittersweet chocolate can be made by combining sweetened chocolate with Baker's bitter chocolate. Use half and half of each, and blend well together before dipping the chocolates in it. Any one who likes the bitter tang in the chocolates may use the bitter chocolate by itself. A small amount of cocoa butter may be added to the melted chocolate; this will make it go further and add to the glossy effect without being harmful.

Melt your chocolate in a double boiler, and always be very careful not to get any water into it or it will not harden, but be messy and sticky. Stir while melting and it will do so more quickly, and the less heat it takes to melt the chocolate the better. After the chocolate is melted it can be placed in bowls or cups for dipping. There are two or three ways of coating chocolate creams. Most confectioners put the chocolate on with their fingers, but if one does not care to do this they can be dipped with a candy dipper or fork into the melted chocolate. They may also be coated with a thin bladed knife or spatula. If you are going to put the chocolate on with the hands it should be allowed to get nearly cool, and then knead well. Only use a small portion at once or it will get too hard, then you must work quickly in a warm room. Use your right hand for coating, and throw the centers into the chocolate with your left. Work the chocolate up around the centers quickly, and then drop on a waxed paper or on clean, smooth tin. String up a little of the chocolate on top and twirl with the fingers to give that twist that is found on most bought creams. For many dipping is much easier. Drop the centers into the melted chocolate, turn over, lift out with wire dipper or fork, with a knife scrape off any surplus chocolate and place on waxed paper or on tin. Set in a cool place immediately to harden. If a knife is used for coating, place a little of the chocolate on oiled or waxed paper, and place the centers on top of it; this forms the bottoms. Then with a knife spread chocolate over the sides, dipping the knife into the chocolate until the centers are entirely coated. If the chocolate hardens before all the creams are dipped it can be melted again.

BONBONS MADE WITH COCOANUT

Cocoanut cubes are made by taking two cupfuls of fondant and melting it in a double boiler, stir in one cupful of grated cocoanut and mix in well. Pour this into a square box lined with paraffine paper; it should be about an inch thick. When cold cut into squares. This cocoanut mixture may be variously tinted and given unusual and elusive flavors, and thus one may have a variety. Another way to make cocoanut cubes is to melt some fondant and pour half of it in a square or oblong box lined with paraffine paper. Then cover this over with cocoanut a half inch, then pour over the remainder of the fondant. This is especially good if the fondant is colored rose or pink. When cold cut into cubes.

A combination of chocolate fondant and cocoanut is excellent. Melt a cupful of chocolate fondant and pour into a square or oblong box lined with paraffine paper. Melt a cup of pink or white fondant in a double boiler and stir in one-half cupful of cocoanut. Pour over the chocolate fondant.

Snowballs can be made by taking one cupful of fondant and melting it, then stir in one-half cupful of grated cocoanut. Form into balls, roll in beaten egg white and then roll in grated cocoanut until thickly covered. Place on paraffine paper until they harden.

Cocoanut drops are made by mixing with two cupfuls of melted fondant one-half cupful of grated cocoanut and one-fourth cupful of finely chopped candied cherries. Add a teaspoonful of juice of maraschino cherries. Drop from a spoon on paraffine paper, and press a candied cherry in the center of each bonbon.

Nut Bonbons

Divide some fondant into four parts. Color one part pink, one part yellow, add to the third violet, and to a fourth green pistachio coloring. Flavor each portion with a different flavoring extract. Take some halved walnut meats and blanch. Form the fondant into round balls the size of hickory-nuts; put a half walnut on each side of the fondant ball and press them together so that the fondant is between the two halves of the walnuts. By using some chocolate fondant, some maple fondant and some white fondant you can have these bonbons in seven colors.

Chop up a half cupful each of almonds, pecans and walnuts and mix with enough fondant to make it of the right consistency to mold into bonbon shape with the hands. Dip in melted maple fondant, or chocolate fondant.

Chop up some almonds fine and mix with some fondant, using about a half cupful of nut meats to each cupful of fondant, flavor with almond, and pour into a square or oblong box lined with paraffine paper. Melt some white fondant and mix with it a half cupful of chopped candied cherries, pour over the nut fondant, and when this has cooled pour over another layer of nut fondant. Cut into cubes and press an almond in some of the cubes and candied cherries in others.

Fruit Bonbons

Remove the stones from nice large dates, fill the cavities with fondant of different flavors and colors. If preferred these may be dipped in fondant, or left as they are. Prunes may be stuffed with fondant or a fondant and nut mixture, and then dipped in fondant of different colors. Chop up some figs until fine, work into this an equal quantity of nut meats. Roll up into balls; if not moist enough add a little cream. Dip into melted fondant. Raisins are also good prepared in this manner. Dip into maple fondant.

Melt some fondant in a double boiler, and stir into it candied orange peel cut into tiny strips. Pour in a lined box or greased square or oblong pan. When partly cool mark off into squares and decorate the top of each square with a tiny star cut out of the candied orange peel. The fondant should be flavored with orange. Candied lemon peel can be used in the same way, and in this case the fondant should be flavored with lemon. When cool cut into squares. Candied cherries can be cut up into bits and stirred into pale pink fondant flavored with rose. Press little hearts cut out of candied cherries in the center of each square.

To make a delicious fruit loaf melt one-half cupful of fondant, add a half teaspoonful extract of almond or vanilla, and stir in two tablespoonfuls of candied cherries cut in quarters, and a tablespoonful of chopped angelica. When mixed pour into a lined candy box in an even layer. Melt one-half cupful of chocolate fondant and stir into it one-fourth cupful of chopped dates and flavor with vanilla. Pour over the other layer in the box. Melt one-half cupful of maple fondant and stir into it one-fourth cupful of chopped nut meats, and pour over the other layers. Cover with paraffine paper and set where it will cool quickly. When firm, break down the sides of the box and cut into slices or cubes. Any kind of fruit may be used in the different layers.

Sections of oranges or tangerines may be dipped in fondant, but one must be careful that they are not broken in any way to let the juice escape as this will probably soften the fondant and make it messy.

Any preserved fruit, dried in the oven, cooled and then dipped in different colored fondant makes delicious bonbons. Preserved strawberries can be dipped in fondant colored pink and flavored with strawberry extract. Preserved cherries can also be dipped in pink or white fondant flavored with almond or cherry. Pears and yellow peaches are good dipped in yellow fondant flavored with lemon or orange. Quince preserves are also good dipped.

Assorted Bonbons

The plain white fondant flavored with vanilla is good dipped in the pink, yellow, green or violet fondant, or in maple fondant; form the white fondant in pretty bonbon shapes before dipping.

Pretty marbles can be made by taking a small piece of two or more colored fondants in the hand and rolling them around until they become smooth and round and beautifully streaked with the different colors. Place on paraffine paper and turn often to prevent their flattening on one side, until firmly set.

Roll out some of the different colored fondant in sheets, place one upon the other, roll gently with the rolling pin until the colors are blended together, then cut into bars or squares.

Form fondant into tiny cones, tucking into each cone a bit of preserved ginger, well dried before using. Dip in different colored fondant. Some can be dipped in melted chocolate also.

Work into a half cupful of fondant one teaspoonful of ground cinnamon, flavor with a drop or two of oil of cinnamon, and form into balls. Dip these in chocolate fondant. Other spice bonbons can be made by using a few drops of the oil of allspice, cloves or nutmeg in flavoring the fondant.

Peppermint and wintergreen wafers can be made by taking some white fondant and coloring it a pale green and flavoring it with peppermint extract. Drop from a spoon on paper the size of a quarter. Wintergreen wafers can be made by coloring the fondant pink and flavoring with wintergreen extract.

Take some fondant and flavor with orange and color a deep yellow; roll out in a long strip about two inches wide. Flavor some more fondant with banana extract and color a light yellow. Form this into a long round stick shape and place in the center of strip. Bring the two edges of the outside fondant together, and press together. Cut off neatly with a knife in half-inch pieces when cool.

How to Dip with Fondant

Just a word in regard to the dipping, and preparing the fondant for dipping. Place the fondant in a double boiler or in a bowl and place the bowl in a saucepan of hot water. The fondant should be melted to about the consistency of thick cream. Be careful that it does not get too hot or it will become a syrup again. Stir occasionally while melting and this will help it to melt not only evenly, but more quickly. If the fondant is very dry a few drops of water may be added, but be very careful not to get too much water in or the bonbons will not harden up well. When ready to dip remove the fondant from the fire, but let the bowl remain in the hot water. Take up the centers to be dipped on a candy dipper or fork and drop into the bowl, then lift them out, scrape off any surplus fondant with a knife, and drop on oiled or waxed paper or smooth tin slightly oiled. These will harden very quickly. One can make a twist on the top of them like the chocolates, but this must be done just as soon as dipped. The fondant can be flavored and colored in any way desired while it is melting.

CHAPTER IX

POP-CORN SWEETS

Excellent, inexpensive and nourishing sweets may be made with popped pop-corn. For making these sweets the pop-corn kernels should be large, crisp and with no hard centers. The best way to pop corn to obtain these results is first to use good pop-corn, then put enough corn in the popper just to cover the bottom of popper. Pour some cold water over it and hold the popper some distance from the heat at first. Continue this for three or four minutes, then place more directly over the heat. The fire over which corn is popped should be hot, even and steady. Shake the popper quickly and steadily until nearly all the grains have popped. When commencing to pop almost every grain should pop open at once. The cold water poured over the corn causes a steam to generate; this makes the corn swell and burst open from the very center in large, crisp, fine flavored kernels. If not ready to make the candy as soon as the corn is popped store in paraffine bags or glass jars and close up tightly, since popped corn soon gets tough if exposed to dampness.

Molasses Pop-Corn Balls

Take one cupful of light brown sugar and one cupful of New Orleans molasses, half a cupful of water and boil to the hard ball stage, then add two tablespoonfuls of butter. Boil to the crack stage, then add a half teaspoonful of soda and pour over some freshly popped corn in a bowl. Stir until the syrup is evenly distributed over the corn, but be careful not to break the grains in doing so. Dip the hands in water, take a portion of the pop-corn up into the hands and press into nice even round balls.

Chocolate Pop-Corn Balls

Pop some corn and pick out only the large crisp, tender grains. Place in a saucepan two cupfuls of granulated sugar, one-half cupful of water and one-fourth teaspoonful of cream of tartar. Boil until it spins a thread or forms a hard ball when dropped in cold water; then flavor with a teaspoonful of vanilla. Pour part of this sugar syrup over the pop-corn, stirring until the syrup is evenly distributed through the pop-corn; while doing this let the remainder stand on the back of the stove. Form into tiny pop-corn balls with the fingers, boil the remaining syrup to the crack stage, then dip each ball into this, and place on paraffine paper until cool. When cool dip into melted sweet chocolate.

Snow Pop-Corn Balls

Take two cupfuls of granulated sugar, one-half cupful of white corn syrup, one-half cupful of water and a pinch of cream of tartar. Boil to the soft ball stage, then flavor with a few drops of peppermint extract or a half teaspoonful of vanilla and pour over the stiffly beaten whites of two eggs. Beat up until light and it begins to harden, then stir in two cupfuls of crisp pop-corn grains. Dip the hands into corn-starch and mold while still warm into small balls. Roll each ball in cocoanut, and then wrap in paraffine paper to keep their shape until cold. Unwrap and heap on plate.

Ice Pop-Corn Balls

Take two cupfuls of granulated sugar, one-half cupful of water and one-fourth teaspoonful of cream of tartar. Boil to the crack stage and pour over pop-corn in a bowl, stirring until the syrup is well mixed with the corn. Form into small balls with the hands. While still warm roll the balls in pulverized or finely chopped rock candy to simulate ice.

Pop-Corn Dainty

Place in a saucepan two cupfuls of granulated sugar, one-half cupful of water and one-fourth teaspoonful of cream of tartar. Boil to firm ball. Just before removing from the fire stir into the syrup a pint of pop-corn that has been run through the food chopper. Pour over the stiffly beaten whites of two eggs, flavor with a teaspoonful of vanilla and beat up until light and foamy; then pour into greased pans, and cut into squares, or drop from a spoon on paraffine paper, and press a whole pop-corn grain into the top of each. These are also nice if crystallized pop-corn in different colors is used for decoration.

Crystallized Pop-Corn

Take two cupfuls of granulated sugar, two tablespoonfuls of white corn syrup and one-half cupful of cream and boil to the soft ball stage. Divide into four portions, pouring each portion on a buttered plate, and flavoring differently with strawberry, orange, maple and melted chocolate respectively. Beat the portion on each plate until creamy, coloring the portion that is flavored with strawberry pink, the orange flavored with yellow. One portion may be left white if liked, or the amount of syrup may be doubled and divided into more portions. Place each kind of the mixture in cups or bowls. Select very large, crisp kernels of corn and dip one by one into the different mixtures until all is used. Dry them on greased or waxed paper. One may use a hat pin to dip with. These grains may be used to decorate other sweets or may be served in little baskets or odd receptacles.

Pop-Corn Bars

Take two cups of sugar, one-half cupful of water and boil to the hard ball stage. Add vanilla flavoring or any desired flavoring. Crush some fresh pop-corn with a rolling pin, and stir into the syrup. When the corn has been perfectly mixed with the syrup press into a square or oblong buttered pan to the depth of about an inch, patting it smooth on top. When cool cut into bars with a very sharp knife.

Maple Pop-Corn Bars

Cook two cupfuls of maple sugar and one cupful of cream to the hard ball stage. Beat up until it begins to turn creamy, then stir in a pint of large, crisp kernels. See that the syrup is well mixed through the corn. Turn into a square or oblong pan that has been well buttered and press until flat on top, but not hard enough to crush the kernels. If liked it can be shaped into bars with the hands, and there will not be so much danger of crushing the kernels. If shaped in a pan cut into bars with a sharp knife.

Pop-Corn Macaroons

Run some freshly popped corn through the food chopper, or else chop up with a knife until fine. To a cupful of these add an equal quantity of blanched almonds that have been pounded to a paste. Put these together in a bowl. Beat up whites of three eggs until stiff, then add about one-half a cupful of sugar and beat up for about five minutes. Mix the pop-corn and paste into this slowly until thoroughly blended. Drop from a spoon on oiled or buttered paper in a pan and sprinkle with powdered sugar. Bake in a moderate oven for about twenty minutes. The centers of these can be decorated with crystallized pop-corn.

Cherokee Crisp

Take two cupfuls of light brown sugar, one-fourth cupful of New Orleans molasses, and one-half cupful of water. Melt over the fire until all the sugar is dissolved, add two tablespoonfuls of butter. Sprinkle some salt over a quart of freshly popped corn in a bowl. Flavor the syrup with a teaspoonful of vanilla after it has reached the hard crack stage and pour over the corn. Turn out on a large platter or marble slab and work until a very thin sheet. When cold break into pieces.

Pop-Corn Almond Nougat

Take two cupfuls of white sugar, one-fourth cupful of water and one-fourth cupful of corn syrup. Melt over the fire until the sugar is dissolved, then stir in one cupful of chopped pop-corn and one-half cupful of chopped almonds. Boil to the hard crack stage, flavor with a little almond extract, and pour over buttered pans in thin sheets. When cold break into pieces or cut into squares with a sharp knife.

MACAROONS AND MISCELLANEOUS SWEETS

Under this head you will find recipes for making macaroons, which are closely allied to candies; and a number of sweets not classified.

Almond Macaroons

To the beaten whites of six eggs add eight ounces of blanched and powdered almonds. With the yolks of the eggs beat one pound of powdered sugar; add the grated rinds of two lemons, a little sliced citron and one-fourth pound of flour, and mix well together. Beat lightly into this the almond whip. Drop from a spoon on greased paper, and bake in a moderate oven until done.

Cream Macaroons

Beat the whites and the yolks of six eggs separately. Add to the yolks three pounds of powdered sugar and the same amount of flour. Add the whites of the eggs and enough flavored whipped cream to mix well; pour into molds, and bake a delicate brown.

Jasmine Macaroons

Into the whites of six eggs beaten until stiff mix one cupful of powdered sugar; then beat into this some jasmine flowers. Make into small cakes, sprinkle with sugar, and bake in a moderate oven.

Queen Macaroons

Mix the beaten whites of six eggs with the yolks of four; add one cupful of sugar and flour and a small quantity of coriander seed. Drop from a spoon on waxed paper and bake in a moderate oven.

Chocolate Macaroons

Take one-fourth pound of grated chocolate, three ounces of blanched and pounded almonds, and a half cupful of granulated or powdered sugar. Mix well together, then make into a soft paste with the stiffly beaten whites of eggs. Drop by teaspoonfuls on greased paper. Bake about one-half hour in a moderate oven.

Cocoanut Macaroons

Take one cup of sugar, two cupfuls of grated cocoanut, and two tablespoonfuls of flour. Blend well together; then make into a paste with the stiffly beaten whites of three eggs.

Hickory-Nut Macaroons

Beat up the whites of three eggs until stiff, add slowly one cup of sifted granulated sugar, or powdered sugar and one cupful of hickory-nut meats chopped fine, and rolled. Bake slowly in a moderate oven until a light brown. If desired these can be flavored with a little vanilla, about a half teaspoonful. All macaroons should be dropped by spoonfuls on greased paper.

Peanut Macaroons

Pass one cupful of peanuts through a food chopper, using the fine cutter. Place in a bowl and add one cupful of powdered sugar, one tablespoonful of flour and blend together into a paste with the whites of two or three eggs beaten until stiff. Drop from a spoon on greased paper and bake in the oven for about thirty minutes or until a light brown in color. A halved peanut can be placed in the center of each macaroon before baking if desired.

Cherry Macaroons

Take a cupful of almonds, chop and rub into a paste, add a cupful of sugar, then add gradually the whites of three eggs. Chop a few candied cherries fine and stir in. Drop from a spoon on buttered paper, place a candied cherry in the center of each macaroon, and bake in a moderate oven.

Coffee Macaroons

Blanch a half pound of almonds and pound to a paste. Mix into this two tablespoonfuls of very strong coffee in liquid form. Use enough coffee to form into a paste; then add the stiffly beaten whites of four eggs and two cupfuls of white sugar. Shape into macaroons, and place on greased or paraffine paper on a pan. Bake for about ten minutes in a hot oven. Decorate the centers with a candied cherry or any candied fruit.

Chocolate Macaroons

Grate four ounces of chocolate very fine and mix with it a tablespoonful of flour, a teaspoonful of cinnamon, one cupful of powdered sugar, and a pinch of cream of tartar. Stir this gradually into the stiffly beaten whites of six eggs, and add a teaspoonful of vanilla. Line pans with oiled or waxed paper and drop by spoonfuls on this, and bake in a slow oven for about twenty or thirty minutes. The centers of these can be decorated with halves of walnut, pecan or hickory-nut meats.

Pistachio Macaroons

Pound a half pound of pistachio nuts to a paste, add to this an equal amount of almond paste, and two cupfuls of sugar. Work into this slowly the stiffly beaten whites of six eggs, or enough to make the paste of the right consistency for macaroons. Bake in a moderate oven. These make pretty pale green macaroons.

Cinnamon Macaroons

Run through a chopper one cupful of almonds, then rub into a paste, mix with an equal quantity of sugar, a tablespoonful of ground cinnamon, one-fourth cupful of finely grated chocolate, then work in carefully the whites of four eggs. Drop on greased paper, and bake in a moderate oven.

Marshmallows

Soak two ounces of gelatine in one-half cupful of water for an hour. Boil two cupfuls of sugar, one-half cup of water, and one-fourth teaspoonful of cream of tartar until it spins a thread. Pour the gelatine on a platter and over this pour the syrup. Beat up for twenty or thirty minutes. Flavor with a teaspoonful of vanilla, if desired, adding it just before the beating up. Pour into well greased cake tin; let stand till solid. Turn out on powdered sugar, cut in squares, and roll in powdered sugar, and keep in a closed jar or box.

Cocoanut Marshmallows

Take two cupfuls of sugar, add a half cupful of water and heat until the sugar is dissolved, then stir in one-half box of gelatine that has been soaked for a few hours in a little water. Let stand until partially cool, then add a pinch of salt, a teaspoonful of vanilla, a cupful and a half of shredded cocoanut, and the stiffly beaten whites of three eggs. Stir well, then pour into deep pans well dusted with corn-starch and powdered sugar. The mixture should be at least a half inch thick. Turn out on powdered sugar and corn-starch, cut into cubes, and roll in the powdered and corn-starch mixture until each marshmallow is well coated, then roll in cocoanut.

Orange Marshmallows

Soak two ounces of gelatine in one cupful of orange juice until dissolved, then strain through cheese-cloth, put into saucepan in a pan of hot water on the stove and add one cup of sugar. Stir the mixture until it is thick and white. Heat until a little stirred on a cold plate will form a creamy ball, remove from the fire and whip into the mixture the stiffly beaten whites of three eggs. Flavor with orange extract, using about a teaspoonful. Whip with silver fork until it begins to thicken. Pour into pan well dusted with corn-starch and powdered sugar; when cool cut in squares and roll in powdered sugar.

Buttercups

Take two cupfuls of granulated sugar, one-half cupful of water and one-half teaspoonful of cream of tartar and boil to the crack stage. Remove from the fire, flavor with one teaspoonful of lemon extract and color yellow with a few drops of yellow fruit or vegetable coloring. When cool enough to handle, pull the yellow candy in a long sheet about two inches wide. In the center of this lay a roll of white or chocolate fondant as long as the strip of candy. Wrap the yellow candy around this fondant, and pull out gently in the hand until you cannot tell where it has been joined. When about cool cut with scissors into lengths of an inch or less.

Hodge-Podge Candy

Place in a bowl one cupful of chopped roasted peanuts, one cupful of chopped pecan meats, one cupful of grated cocoanut, one-half cupful of finely chopped citron, one-fourth cupful each of candied orange and lemon peel, two teaspoonfuls of vanilla and two tablespoonfuls of lemon juice. Take two cupfuls of brown sugar, one cupful of granulated sugar, one cupful of molasses, and one-half teaspoonful of salt. Boil to the soft ball stage, then add two squares of chocolate and a tablespoonful of butter. Boil to the hard ball stage, add one teaspoonful of vanilla, then pour over the nut and fruit mixture in the bowl. Stir until it begins to get creamy and thick, then put into the pans quickly, spreading it even with a spoon. Mark off into squares, and when cool cut. This can be varied by adding different kinds of fruits and nuts.

Candied Sweet Potato Balls

Take some good sweet potatoes, peel them, and then scoop out little balls with a vegetable scoop. Boil these balls in slightly salted water until tender enough to pierce with a splint. Remove from the fire and drain off the water. Take two cupfuls of sugar and one-half cupful of water and cook to a thick syrup, add a teaspoonful of vanilla and part of the potato balls, dropping them in carefully to prevent breaking. Let them simmer until they are coated with a thick coating and are transparent or clear. Remove one at a time with a skimmer or fork, and drop on paraffine paper. These should harden up on the outside, and make a delicious confection.

Persian Confection

Take two cupfuls of granulated sugar and dissolve in one-half cupful of pineapple juice. Place over the fire in a double boiler, and when it boils add an ounce of best gelatine that has been soaked in a little water. Cook for twenty minutes, then stir in one cupful of finely chopped dates and one-half cupful of finely chopped almonds. Stir well, then pour into a pan dusted with corn-starch and powdered sugar. Let stand for twelve hours, and then cut into squares and roll in powdered sugar.

Turkish Confection

Take two cupfuls of granulated sugar and one-half cupful of water, place in a double boiler and bring to a boil, then add one ounce of best gelatine (pink or red gelatine can be used) that has been dissolved in a half cupful of cold water. Bring to the boiling point and let it simmer for twenty minutes. Remove from the fire and add one cupful of orange juice, two tablespoonfuls of lemon juice, the grated rind of one orange, and the grated rind of one-half lemon. Dust a pan with corn-starch and powdered sugar, pour in the mixture and let stand for about twelve hours or until perfectly cool and firm. Cut into cubes and dust with powdered sugar.

Arabian Confection

Take two cupfuls of granulated sugar, one-fourth teaspoonful of cream of tartar and one-half cupful of water. Boil to the soft ball stage, then add two ounces of best gelatine which has been soaked in three-fourths cupful of water for about two hours or until dissolved, juice of one lemon and one cupful of finely chopped figs, or figs and dates mixed. Stir until the mixture thickens, then pour into pan dusted with corn-starch and powdered sugar to an inch or half inch in depth. Let stand until perfectly cool and firm, then cut into cubes and dust with powdered sugar.

Honeycomb Candy

Place in a saucepan two cupfuls of granulated sugar, one-half cupful of water, one tablespoonful of butter and two teaspoonfuls of cream of tartar. Boil to the hard ball stage. Just before removing from the fire add one teaspoonful of vanilla or any flavoring desired, and a little coloring if you wish a colored candy. Pour on a buttered plate or pan, and when cool enough to handle pull quickly with ends of fingers. Stretch out on board to harden. Cut into strips. If rightly made this candy will look like honeycomb, being porous and brittle when cold.

Turkish Delight

Soak the contents of a box of granulated gelatine in two-thirds cupful of orange juice for fifteen minutes. Take off the fire, add the juice of a lemon, one-half cupful of preserved pears, one-half cupful of candied ginger and candied lemon peel combined. Pour into a pan dusted with a mixture of corn-starch and powdered sugar. Let stand until cool, then cut in cubes.

Apple Sweetmeats

Grate two large white raw apples into the unbeaten whites of two eggs, beat up until thick and stiff, then gradually add one cupful of sugar. Dissolve two tablespoonfuls of gelatine in a half pint of good cream, sweeten to taste, and when cool beat up until light and firm and snow white. Fold the apple mixture into the whipped cream and pour into molds. Roll in powder after the bonbons have been turned out of the molds.

Chocolate Arabics

Melt in a double boiler a cake of unsweetened chocolate. Melt in a bowl some fondant flavored with any preferred flavoring. Buy some gum-drops and dip these in the fondant and place on paraffine paper to harden; then dip in the melted chocolate. A little vanilla can be added to the melted chocolate. By dipping gum-drops in this manner their character is entirely changed, and much improved.

Oriental Bonbons

Soak a half pound of gum arabic in two cupfuls of water until soft. Stir into it two cupfuls of confectioner's sugar and cook over the fire in a double boiler until an opaque thick mass. When it forms a firm ball remove from fire and stir in the stiffly beaten whites of two eggs, one-half cupful of orange jelly and one-half cupful of grated cocoanut. Make depressions in a pan of corn-starch and pour a little of the mixture into each depression. When cool remove and dust with powdered sugar.

Candy Potatoes

Take two cupfuls of granulated sugar, one-half cupful of water, and one-fourth teaspoonful of cream of tartar. Boil to the soft ball stage. Work into this one-half cupful of nut meats that have been pounded to a paste and one-half cupful of grated cocoanut. Pour on a platter or marble slab and work with a spoon until it is cool enough to work with the hands, and then knead until it is like dough. Sprinkle some ground cinnamon on a sheet of waxed paper. Take pieces of this dough and form into potato shape. Roll in the cinnamon. Lay on paper until firm.

Divinity Hash

Take two cupfuls of granulated sugar, one-half cupful of maple sugar, one-half cupful of golden corn syrup, and a cupful of water, add a pinch of cream of tartar. Boil to the soft ball stage. Add one teaspoonful of vanilla, and pour over the stiffly beaten whites of two eggs. Have ready one pound of chopped fruit, nuts and grated cocoanut and stir in just before it is ready to pour into buttered pans. After pouring the syrup over the whites of eggs beat up until light and foamy. Any kind of fruit, such as dates, citron, figs, raisins, candied cherries and orange and lemon peel can be used, and also any kinds of nuts. This is a hash, but a delicious one.

CHAPTER XI

CAKE CONFECTIONERY AND LITTLE SWEETS

Delicious bonbons may be made with cake and fondant, and then there are many little sweets that are so closely allied to candies that they may well be included in a book on candy-making. To make these confections one needs to have fancy little cake cutters of all kinds, such as heart, star, round, diamond, leaf, bird and animal shapes. If these are not readily obtained a tinsmith will make them for you if you tell him just what you desire. You will also need a pastry bag with a finely pointed tube, and tiny gem pans.

Bonbon Cakes

The cakes that are best for making bonbons are the sponge cake, pound cake and angel food cake: these should be at least twenty-four hours old, and then can be cut up into any shape desired without breaking or crumbling. Scoop out little balls, using a vegetable scoop, from any of these cakes and dip in melted fondant flavored with different flavors and colored in different colors. If you are planning a luncheon or entertainment it is nice to have these little cake bonbons to help carry out the color scheme. Angel food cake cut in fancy shapes and dipped into pink or rose fondant flavored with rose extract is good. Sponge cake is nice dipped into yellow fondant flavored with orange or lemon, or into chocolate fondant.

These little cake bonbons can be made with delicious fillings. Cut a sheet of angel food cake, which should be about an inch thick, into tiny hearts. With a small round cutter remove the center of each, leaving the bottom one-fourth inch thick. Fill this little hollow with candied pineapple or any candied fruit mixed with a little fondant, or with chopped nuts worked into a little fondant. Then dip in red or pink fondant; these are nice for St. Valentine's day or for bridal occasions. Take some sponge cake and cut into slices about an inch thick, cut out with a small star-shaped cutter.

Cut out half-way through with a smaller star cutter. Fill these hollows in with a chocolate custard. Spread a little white of egg on edges of stars, and place two stars together, then dip in yellow fondant, or chocolate fondant. Dip these little cakes in the fondant with a fork just as you would other bonbons and drop on paraffine paper to harden.

Little rose confections can be made by dipping small round cakes in rose colored fondant, and laying on top of each a few candied rose petals, arranged to look like a rose. Violet confections can be made by cutting small round cakes out of angel food cake, dipping them in violet fondant and decorating the top with candied violets.

Cut tiny stars out of a thin sheet of angel food cake or pound cake, dip in white fondant, and cover the tops over with the tiny silver or gold coated confectionery that one can obtain at the confectionery shops, and you will have silver and gold stars, which will be nice for Christmas. Cut some sponge cake or pound cake into little squares, dip into melted maple fondant, and decorate the top with halved walnuts, pecans or almonds. Cut some sponge or pound cake into slices an inch thick, then cut into cubes, make a little slit in one side, slip in a bit of preserved ginger, candied citron or orange rind. Dip in yellow fondant flavored with lemon or orange. Cut out some sponge cake to resemble sections of orange. Dip in orange fondant flavored with orange.

Little heart shaped cakes dipped in pink or white fondant and then decorated in the center with little hearts cut out of candied cherries are nice. Squares or rounds of angel food cake dipped in fondant, and pressed with some sort of die, say a wish-bone, horseshoe, swastika or flower, then the impression made filled in with a different colored fondant carefully piped in with the pastry bag, are unique.

Cut out some of the cake with a leaf-shaped cutter. Dip into a leaf-green fondant flavored with pistachio, and you will have pretty cakes. The leaf can be veined with chocolate put on with the pastry bag and pipe.

Cut out some sponge cake in shape of dominoes, dip in white fondant, and then mark the dots as in dominoes with melted chocolate.

Slice some sponge cake a fourth of an inch thick, and cut out with a cutter in small rounds. On one-half of these cakes spread jelly of different kinds, such as peach, currant, and raspberry. Put the unspread cakes on these, and cover with fondant. In flavoring the fondant use what combines with the jelly used—almond flavoring with the peach jelly, chocolate with currant and so on. Use differently colored fondants and they will look very pretty.

Spice Nuts

Take two eggs, one cupful of granulated sugar, one-fourth cupful of almond meats, one-fourth cupful of citron, one-half teaspoonful each of cinnamon, allspice and cloves, one cupful of flour, and one teaspoonful of baking-powder. Cut the nuts and citron up very fine. Sift the flour and baking-powder together and mix with the nuts, fruit and spices. Beat up the eggs and sugar until light and thick, then gradually add the flour mixture. The dough should be stiff enough so that it can be formed into little balls about the size of a hickory-nut. If too stiff add a little water, if not stiff enough add a little more flour to make it of the right consistency. Drop on buttered tins about an inch apart and bake in the oven until a light brown.

Chocolate Nuts

Take one cupful of flour and add to it one tablespoonful of baking-powder. Sift into a bowl and add one cupful of sugar. Mix well together. Melt one-half cupful of grated chocolate in a tablespoonful of hot water, add two teaspoonfuls of vanilla and half a teaspoonful of soda. Beat up two eggs, add the chocolate and one-fourth cupful of melted butter. Work into the flour and sugar mixture. The dough must be stiff enough to form into balls the size of a hickory-nut. Drop on greased tins an inch apart. When cool dip in chocolate fondant.

Walnut Wafers

Cream one cupful of butter with one and one-half cupfuls of sugar; add three beaten eggs; put two cupfuls of chopped walnut meats into one cupful of flour, and add this to the batter. Sift one teaspoonful of baking-powder and one and one-half cupfuls of flour together, and add at the last. Drop by spoonfuls on buttered tins, dust with granulated sugar, and put a whole walnut meat on each one. Bake them in a moderate oven.

Peanut Jumbles

Take two tablespoonfuls of butter, one cupful of sugar, one egg, half a teaspoonful of soda, one teaspoonful of cream of tartar, one tablespoonful of milk, and flour enough to make a soft dough. Roll thin and cut with a jumble cutter, brush over with beaten egg and cover lightly with chopped peanuts. Bake separately the small rounds cut from the center.

Cocoanut Jumbles

Beat half a cupful of butter and half a cupful of sugar to a cream, flavor with a teaspoonful of vanilla, then add two eggs, a cupful of freshly grated cocoanut, and two cupfuls of flour sifted with a level teaspoonful of baking-powder. Pat and roll out thin on a well-floured board, adding more flour if needed. Flour a jumble cutter well and cut into rings. Brush the tops of the cakes with milk and sprinkle with a mixture of granulated sugar and cocoanut. Place far enough apart on buttered pan so that they will not touch when baked. Bake in a rather hot oven until a pale brown.

Fruit Rocks

Cream one cup of sugar with two-thirds cup of butter, add one and a half cupfuls of flour, two eggs, one cupful of English walnut meats, one cupful of chopped raisins, one teaspoonful of cinnamon, one teaspoonful of cream of tartar and one-half teaspoonful of soda dissolved in a little water. Drop by teaspoonfuls on buttered tins an inch or more apart. Press one-half of an English walnut meat or a raisin in the center of each, and bake until a nice brown.

Raisin Spirals

Take one cup of sugar, one-half cupful of butter and yolks of two eggs, and beat to a cream. Add one cupful of sour milk and one cupful of chopped raisins; one-half teaspoonful each of cinnamon and nutmeg. Dissolve one teaspoonful of soda in a little of the milk. Just before putting in the flour add the beaten whites of two eggs. Make a very stiff dough and cut into thin strips about five inches long. Roll around the finger and fry in butter a delicate brown.

Fruit Bars

Mix together one cupful of butter and one cupful of brown sugar until creamy, add two well-beaten eggs, one-half cupful of sour milk and scant teaspoonful of soda if the milk is thoroughly sour, if not use only half a teaspoonful. Beat up together, then add enough flour to make a dough that will roll nicely but be careful not to get it too stiff. Flour the board well, then roll out thin and cut with a narrow oblong cutter. Put through a food chopper one pound of stoned dates and one-half pound of figs. Work together and then roll in a thin sheet. Put a layer of this fruit paste between every two of the cakes in sandwich fashion. Bake in a hot oven. Marmalades or candied fruits or nut and fruit mixtures can be used for these bars.

Maple Drops

To a half cupful of maple syrup add one teaspoonful of melted butter, one well-beaten egg and one cup of flour sifted with a teaspoonful of baking-powder. Add a pinch of salt. Beat and drop by spoonfuls or half-spoonfuls on buttered tin, and bake in a quick oven. Cover with maple fondant.

Ginger Chips

Stir together a cupful of butter and one cupful of brown sugar. Add one tablespoonful of ginger and one teaspoonful each of cloves and cinnamon. Mix in two cupfuls of good baking molasses and the grated peel of a large lemon. Add a teaspoonful of soda dissolved in a little hot water. Mix in enough flour to make a stiff paste. Roll out very thin, a small portion at a time, and cut into narrow strips about one inch wide and four inches long. Bake in a moderate oven for ten minutes.

Ginger Wafers

Stir one-fourth cupful of butter and one-half cupful of sugar to a cream, add two eggs, the whites and yolks beaten separately. Add a half cupful of flour or just enough to make a thin batter, mix well, then add one tablespoonful of ginger, and the grated peel of a lemon. Drop by spoonfuls on buttered tins, far enough apart not to run together. Bake in a moderate oven, and when half done roll up into little cylinders, and return to the oven and crisp until brown.

Marshmallow Cakes

Blanch and dry gently in the open oven sufficient hickory-nut meats to fill three-fourths of a cup. Cool and chop very finely. Beat three eggs, yolks and whites together, until light. Add the nuts, two tablespoonfuls of powdered sugar, a half teaspoonful of orange extract and sufficient flour to form a soft dough. Roll out on board until about an inch in thickness and cut in small diamonds that measure only two or three inches from point to point. Lay on shallow greased tins and bake to a pale brown in a moderate oven. Frost with marshmallow icing while they are still warm.

Ginger Nuts

Take one pint of baking molasses and add one-half cupful of melted butter, one cupful of brown sugar and one tablespoonful of powdered ginger. Stir these ingredients well together, and while mixing add two tablespoonfuls of candied lemon or orange peel, one tablespoonful of candied angelica cut into small dice, and a teaspoonful of soda dissolved in a little warm water. Having mixed all thoroughly together break in one egg and work in as much flour to form a paste just stiff enough to handle. Form into balls, and press a raisin or blanched almond in the top of each, and bake on greased tins in a rather quick oven.

German Ginger Balls

Beat up four eggs until very light and foamy; then add gradually a half pound of light brown sugar, a teaspoonful of ginger, and one-half teaspoonful of allspice or cinnamon, the juice of one lemon and three-fourths cupful of pastry flour. Form with floured hands into small balls, placing in the center of each a tiny piece of preserved ginger, or candied ginger. Place in a greased baking-pan far enough apart not to touch when baked. Bake in a quick oven.

Cinnamon Crisps

Beat one-third cup of butter and two-thirds cup of sugar until light and creamy, then add one teaspoonful of ground cinnamon, one and one-half cups of flour and one teaspoonful of baking-powder together. Mix to a dough with one-third cup of milk, using only enough to make the dough so that it will roll out easily. Roll very thin, and cut into small squares or rounds. Bake on greased tins in a moderate oven.

Chocolate Sticks

Cream together one cupful of sugar, one tablespoonful of butter, the yolk of one egg and one-half cup of milk. Melt one and one-half squares of chocolate, add to the mixture, then add one cupful of flour, add one-half cupful more of milk, and one-fourth cupful of flour into which has been sifted one teaspoonful baking-powder and one-fourth teaspoonful of soda. Bake in a sheet that will be about three-fourths of an inch thick when baked. Cut into strips about one inch wide and three or four inches long. When cool dip into pink fondant, then into melted chocolate. Decorate the top of each strip with a half of a pecan or hickory-nut meat.

Orange Cakes

Cream together one-half cupful of butter, one cup of sugar, add the yolks of five eggs beaten thick, one-half cupful of milk, one and three-fourths cupfuls of flour sifted with two level teaspoonfuls of baking-powder. Add one teaspoonful of orange extract. Roll out and cut in star or other fancy shape. Cover with yellow orange flavored fondant, and sprinkle over the top with candied orange peel cut into bits.

Cocoanut Drops

Sift together one and one-half cupfuls of flour and a rounding teaspoonful of baking-powder. Beat up one egg until light, then beat into it one-half cupful of sugar, add a half cupful of grated cocoanut and a teaspoonful of grated lemon rind, then alternately the flour and half a cupful of rich cream. Drop in little pats on greased pans which have been dusted with flour. Have the cakes far enough apart so that the batter will not run together. Sprinkle a little grated cocoanut over the top of each cake and bake in a moderate oven.

Almond Cakes

Mix together one-fourth cupful of butter and a cupful of sugar to a cream, add the beaten yolks of four eggs, one-fourth cupful of cream and two cupfuls of flour in which has been placed one teaspoonful of baking-powder. Roll out on a well-floured board about one-fourth of an inch thick, cover with powdered sugar and cut into diamonds. Spread with maple fondant, and sprinkle the cakes thickly with blanched and chopped almonds.

Peanut Wafers

Beat together one-half cupful of nice white lard mixed with butter (half and half of each) and one cupful of sugar, add one cupful of ground peanuts, and one and one-half cupfuls of flour mixed together with one teaspoonful of baking-powder, and one-third teaspoonful of salt. Add one-half cupful of milk or water, or just enough to make a dough that will roll thinly. It is best to mix the flour and milk in alternately. Cut into small rounds and place a half peanut meat on top of each cake.

German Wafers

Warm one-third cupful of butter, and stir in five eggs, one at a time. Mix in one quart of sifted flour, and one teaspoonful each of vanilla and banana extract. Spread over a buttered dripping pan and bake in a hot oven until a delicate brown. Cut into squares, pick with a fork and dip into powdered sugar.

Japanese Wafers

Beat up the whites of two eggs until stiff, then add two tablespoonfuls of rice flour and two tablespoonfuls of sugar. Work in one tablespoonful of softened butter. Pour into a pan lined with paraffine or oiled paper, making it as thin as possible. Bake in a moderate oven and roll around a round stick, after cutting them in four inch squares.

English Wafers

Stir together one cupful of butter with one-half cupful of sugar, add four eggs, the whites and yolks beaten separately, one-half cupful of currants, and one-fourth teaspoonful of cinnamon. Add two tablespoonfuls of strong rose water and three-fourths cup of flour, roll very thin and bake on buttered tins for about five minutes or until a delicate brown; cut into small squares, and dust with powdered sugar.

Delicious Tea Cookies

Cream together one-half cupful of butter and one cupful of sugar, add four eggs, one cupful of chopped nut meats, one cupful of chopped raisins, a teaspoonful of soda stirred in one cupful of good New Orleans molasses, and one-half teaspoonful each of cinnamon and allspice. Add enough flour to make a dough that will roll out thin. Mix all the ingredients well together. Bake in a hot oven and ice or not as liked.

Raisin Cookies

Cream together one cupful of butter and one cupful of sugar, add two eggs well beaten; then add one teaspoonful of soda and two teaspoonfuls of cream of tartar dissolved in a little lukewarm water. Now stir in three cupfuls of flour, one cupful of chopped raisins, one teaspoonful of cinnamon, and one-fourth teaspoonful of nutmeg. Drop the batter in spoonfuls on a well-buttered pan, being careful to leave room for the cakes to spread. Bake in a moderate oven until a nice brown color.

Love Diamonds

Cream together one cupful of sugar and one-fourth cupful of butter, then add one-half cupful of sweet milk. Sift with one cupful of flour one teaspoonful of baking-powder and add half of it. Stir in two whites of eggs beaten stiff, and then the remainder of the flour and a teaspoonful of vanilla. Pour into a square pan and bake. When cool cut into diamonds. Mix into a cupful of melted chocolate fondant a half cupful of cocoanut, and spread the diamonds with this, or spread with a pink fondant flavored with rose, and sprinkled over with grated cocoanut.

Marmalade Diamonds

Cream together one-half cupful of butter and one cupful of granulated sugar; then add the beaten yolks of three eggs, one-half cupful of sweet milk; then work in two cupfuls of flour into which has been sifted two teaspoonfuls of baking-powder, add the stiffly beaten whites of three eggs and one teaspoonful of lemon extract. Pour into square pan and bake. When cool cut into diamonds. On half of the cakes spread lemon, orange or any good marmalade, and place the other halves on these in sandwich fashion. Cover with yellow fondant flavored with lemon or orange.

Lemon Cakes

Cream together one cupful of butter and one cupful of sugar, add two eggs, one teaspoonful of soda dissolved in two tablespoonfuls of sweet milk, and the grated rind and juice of one lemon. Add enough flour to knead into a stiff dough, roll thin, cut into stars, rounds or squares. Bake in a quick oven. Ice with lemon flavored fondant or icing.

Maple Nut Wafers

Cream together one cupful of maple sugar and one-half cupful of butter, add two eggs, the whites and yolks beaten separately. Sift and add two thirds cupful of flour and one-half cupful of chopped nut meats. Sift in the flour one teaspoonful of baking-powder. The batter should be of the right consistency to spread thinly over a buttered pan; if too stiff add a little milk.

Sprinkle over the top with coarse chopped nuts. Bake rather slowly and cut into squares before removing from the oven.

Vanilla Wafers

Cream together one-third cupful of butter and one cupful of sugar, add one egg, and one-fourth cup of sweet milk. Sift together one teaspoonful of salt, one teaspoonful of baking-powder, with two and one-fourth cupfuls of flour. Beat up, add a tablespoonful of vanilla. Pour into pan, spreading thinly over it. Bake in a moderate oven.

Chocolate Diamonds

Cream together one-half cupful of butter and one cupful of sugar. Sift into three cupfuls of pastry flour two tablespoonfuls of baking-powder, then add alternately with one cupful of sweet milk, and two eggs. Flavor with one teaspoonful of vanilla. Bake in square layer cake tins, and when cold cut into diamonds. On the half of these cakes spread a chocolate paste made as follows: Beat some fresh butter with a wooden spoon until it is soft and creamy. Add by degrees sufficient milk chocolate, which has been reduced to a very fine powder, to make the butter quite brown. Flavor with vanilla. Place the unspread cakes on top of the spread ones in sandwich fashion, and ice with chocolate fondant, or else use white fondant and sprinkle thickly with chopped almonds.

Coriander Cakes

Cream together one cupful of sugar and four eggs until thick and white, then add one and a half cupfuls of flour into which has been sifted one teaspoonful of baking-powder; then add two tablespoonfuls of coriander seed and one teaspoonful of lemon extract. This should be a rather thick sponge. Drop by spoonfuls on buttered pans or greased paper. Bake in a hot oven to a golden brown.

Peach Blossom Cakes

Cream together one cupful of sugar and one-half cupful of butter, then add one-half cupful of sweet milk. Sift into one cupful and a half of flour two teaspoonfuls of baking-powder and stir in half of this, then add the stiffly beaten whites of three eggs and then the remainder of the flour and one-half teaspoonful of corn-starch. Pour into two square pans and bake in a rather quick oven. When cool cut in small squares and ice with pink fondant flavored with peach or rose extract or ice with white fondant and sprinkle with pink pulverized sugar.

Wild Rose Cakes

Cream together one-half cupful of butter and one cupful of sugar, then add one-half cupful of sweet milk. Sift with one teaspoonful of baking-powder into one cupful of flour, add part of the flour, then the stiffly beaten whites of three eggs, then add the remainder of the flour and a teaspoonful of rose or strawberry extract. Beat up thoroughly and bake in sheets in two square pans. Cut into squares when cool and ice with white fondant, and then with a pastry tube and pink fondant place a wild rose in the center of each cake. Put a little yellow or chocolate fondant in the center of each rose.

Cream Nut Puffs

Take one-half cupful of butter, one and one-half cupfuls of flour, eight eggs and two cupfuls of hot water. Melt the butter in the water, set over the fire and bring to a gentle boil. Then put in the flour and boil until it leaves the sides of the saucepan, never ceasing to stir. One minute is enough. Turn into a bowl to cool. Beat the eggs in one at a time, beating one minute after each egg is put in, and then when all are in beat for two or three minutes. Set on ice for an hour, then drop in spoonfuls on buttered paper, being careful to get them far enough apart so that they will not touch each other. Bake for about fifteen minutes in a quick oven or until a nice brown. When cool make a slit in the side of each and fill with a cream nut filling made as follows: Place in a double boiler one cupful of milk, stir into this a tablespoonful of corn-starch dissolved in a little milk, and gradually one egg beaten light and one-half cupful of sugar. Stir until thick and smooth, then stir in one-half cupful of finely chopped hickory or pecan nut meats.

Flavor with a teaspoonful of vanilla. When cold fill into the slits in the cakes. These are delicious.

Spice Fingers

Beat five eggs and two cupfuls of light brown sugar until light, then stir in one teaspoonful of cinnamon and one-half teaspoonful each of cloves, allspice and nutmeg, also one-fourth cupful of almonds pounded into a paste and two ounces of citron cut fine; then add one-half cupful of molasses, and lastly the flour into which three level teaspoonfuls of baking-powder have been sifted. Use enough flour to make it stiff enough to roll thin. Cut into long strips about the length of a finger, and about an inch wide. Bake on greased pan in a moderate oven. When cool dip into chocolate fondant or any colored fondant. They are good dipped into maple fondant.

Caraway Cookies

Cream together one cupful of sugar, one-half cupful of butter till light, then add one-fourth cup of water, and two eggs well beaten. Sift with three cupfuls of flour two teaspoonfuls of baking-powder, and add gradually, and then stir in a tablespoonful of caraway seeds. Mix the ingredients well together, roll thin and cut out in fancy shapes or in rounds. Bake in the oven until a delicate brown.

Daisy Cakes

Cream together one-fourth cup of butter and two-thirds cupful of sugar, add one egg, one-half cupful of cold water or sweet milk, and the grated rind of one orange. Sift a teaspoonful of baking-powder with one cupful of flour and stir in. Beat steadily for five or eight minutes, then turn into small greased gem pans. Bake in a moderate oven. Turn out of the pans and when cold cover with orange fondant. With halved almonds form a daisy in the center of each cake, using a center of candied orange peel.

Vanilla Sugar Cakes

Cream together one cupful of butter and one cupful of sugar, add two well-beaten eggs, and three teaspoonfuls of vanilla extract. Sift with three cupfuls of flour three teaspoonfuls of baking-powder. Roll out thin, sprinkle with sugar and press in with the rolling pin. Cut into rounds or squares and bake them a delicate brown on greased tins.

Chocolate Ginger Drops

Place in a bowl one cupful of molasses, half a cupful of sour cream, one tablespoonful (level) of ginger, one teaspoonful of cinnamon and mix well together, then stir in one-fourth cupful of melted butter. Dissolve a teaspoonful of soda in a little water and add to the other ingredients. Add enough sifted flour to make a drop batter. Drop from spoon on greased pan, far enough not to touch each other when baked. Dip each little drop cake into melted chocolate fondant. The dough should be stiff enough so that the batter will not run over the pan but keep its shape when baked. Try a bit of the batter in the oven before putting in the cakes. These cakes should be baked in a quick oven.

Cocoanut Fruit Drops

Cream together one cup of sugar and one-half cup of butter, then add one egg and one cup of milk. Mix one cupful of raisins in one-half cupful of flour and add to the other ingredients with one and one-half cupfuls of flour into which has been sifted two teaspoonfuls of baking-powder, then add one-half cupful of grated cocoanut and one teaspoonful of vanilla. Drop by spoonfuls on greased pans and bake in a moderate oven fifteen minutes. Can be iced with white fondant and sprinkled over with grated cocoanut.

Preserved Fruit Dainties

Cream together one-half cupful of butter and one cupful of sugar, then add three well-beaten eggs and one-half cupful of sweet milk. Mix smooth and then add gradually one and a half cupfuls of flour into which has been sifted one teaspoonful of baking-powder. The dough should be as soft as it can be handled easily. Flour the board well and cut out into rounds or squares, and place preserved fruit over the top. Any thick preserved fruit may be used. Bake in a quick oven a nice brown.

Jelly Jumbles

Cream together one-half cupful of butter and one cup of sugar, add one well-beaten egg, then one and one-half cupfuls of flour into which have been sifted one teaspoonful of baking-powder and one-fourth teaspoonful of salt. Stir well, then add one-third cup of sweet milk or just enough to form a dough that will roll out. Flour the board and roll very thin. Cut out with a jumble cutter or a doughnut cutter. Spread half of these with some good jelly, and place the unspread cakes on top of these in sandwich fashion. Press the edges slightly together and bake on greased pans.

Chocolate Nut Wafers

Cream together one-half cupful of butter with one cupful of sugar, add two well-beaten eggs, and two squares of grated chocolate melted in one-fourth cupful of hot water. Sift with two-thirds cup of flour one teaspoonful of baking-powder, and a pinch of soda. Pour very thinly over well-greased pans, and sprinkle generously over with chopped nut meats. Bake in a moderate oven, and cut into small squares or diamonds.

Lady Fingers

Beat five eggs up until light, add one-half cupful of powdered sugar and beat up for several minutes; sift in with one cupful of flour one teaspoonful of baking-powder and stir slowly. Place the batter in a pastry bag and run it out through the tube on light brown paper (not buttered), making each cake about a finger in length, and about one-fourth inch wide; be careful not to get them too wide. Sprinkle with granulated sugar, bake in a quick oven. Place the paper on a damp table and let stand a few moments and the cakes can be readily removed. Stick the cakes together back to back; this will make them round like fingers. If liked a little jelly may be spread between the cakes before putting them together.

Fruit Puffs

Take five eggs and beat the whites and yolks separately, stir in gradually one and a half cupfuls of sugar, and one and a half cupfuls of flour into which has been sifted two teaspoonfuls of baking-powder. Bake in deep gem pans, filling about half full. Make a fruit filling as follows: Place in a saucepan one-half cupful of finely chopped figs, one-half cupful of dates, one-half cupful of chopped raisins and one-half cupful of water. Let simmer slowly for an hour, then add a teaspoonful of vanilla. Make slits in the sides of the cakes and fill in with this fruit mixture. Cover with icing or chocolate fondant.

Nut Tarts

Prepare a short pastry crust, adding to the flour one tablespoonful of powdered sugar. Roll out very thin. Dip fancy cutters in flour and cut the pastry, then pierce the half of the cakes with a small circular cutter. Some of the cakes can be made with one hole, some two and some three. Place these on greased pans and bake in the oven a pale brown. After removing make a paste with the stiffly beaten whites of two eggs, two tablespoonfuls of finely chopped nut meats, two tablespoonfuls of maple sugar, and a little cream if the paste is too thick to spread nicely. Spread this on the cakes that have been left whole, and then place the cakes with the holes on top. Fill up the depressions or holes with jelly, marmalade or fondant.

End

www.ingramcontent.com/pod-product-compliance
Lightning Source LLC
Chambersburg PA
CBHW081125080526
44587CB00021B/3751